HENRY WADSWORTH LONGFELLOW
America's Beloved Poet

World Writers

HENRY WADSWORTH LONGFELLOW
America's Beloved Poet

Bonnie L. Lukes

MORGAN
REYNOLDS
Incorporated

Greensboro

HENRY WADSWORTH LONGFELLOW *America's Beloved Poet*

Photos courtesy of the National Park Service, Longfellow Historical Site and the Collections
of the Maine Historical Society.

Library of Congress Cataloging-in-Publication Data
Lukes, Bonnie L.
  Henry Wadsworth Longfellow : America's beloved poet / Bonnie L. Lukes.
      p. cm.
  Includes bibliographical references and index.
  Summary: A biography of one of the major American poets of the nineteenth century,
whose works include "The Song of Hiawatha" and "The Village Blacksmith."
    ISBN 1-883846-31-5
      1. Longfellow, Henry Wadsworth, 1807-1882—Biography—Juvenile literature.
  2. Poets, American—19th century—Biography—Juvenile literature. [1. Longfellow, Henry
  Wadsworth, 1807-1882. 2. Poets, American.] I. Title.
  PS2281.L85 1998
  811'.3—dc21
  [B]

                                                          98-7934
                                                            CIP
                                                            AC

Printed in the United States of America
First Edition

Dedicated to—
Cassie, Chad, Sarah and Natalie,
who make every day a poem to be sung.

CONTENTS

Chapter One:
  "Long, Long Thoughts of Youth" 9
Chapter Two
  "I Will Be Eminent in Something" 20
Chapter Three
  "I Have Reached the Shores of the Old World" 32
Chapter Four
  "Good Fortune" and "Sorrow Unspeakable" 42
Chapter Five
  "Voices of the Night" 54
Chapter Six
  "O, Day Forever Blessed" 64
Chapter Seven
  "The Air is Full of Farewells" 73
Chapter Eight
  "I Have Delivered My Last Lecture" 79
Chapter Nine
  "Sorrow Seeks Out Such Days As These" 85
Chapter Ten
  "Aftermath" 97
Chapter Eleven
  "As the Evening Twilight Fades" 105
Notes 110
Major Works 114
Timeline 115
Sources 117
Bibliography 124
Index 125

Henry Wadsworth Longfellow

Chapter One

"Long, Long Thoughts of Youth"

Thirteen-year-old Henry Longfellow stood watching his father read the *Portland Gazette*. Henry shifted from foot to foot. Several days earlier, he had slipped a poem into the *Gazette* editor's mailbox—a poem he himself had written. He felt he could not wait a second longer to see if the newspaper had printed his poem. But he dared not interrupt his father's reading.

Finally, Mr. Longfellow laid the paper aside and left the room without comment. Henry's shoulders sagged. The editor must not have liked his poem. But perhaps his father had skipped over it. It had, after all, been signed only "Henry."

Quickly, he opened the paper to the "Poet's Corner." And there it was! His poem. He read the title aloud: "The Battle of Lovell's Pond." He read each line, savoring every word. Throughout the day, Henry re-read the poem again and again. Only his sister, Anne, knew he had written it. She would keep his secret until he was ready to announce his triumph to the rest of the family.

That evening Henry visited his friend, Frederic. Shortly after Henry arrived, Frederic's father, Judge Mellen, asked if anyone had seen the poem in that day's paper. The poem, he said, was a "very stiff piece—remarkably stiff; moreover, it is all borrowed, every word of it." Henry cringed. The words cut like a knife, and "he would gladly have sunk through the floor." Terrified that the judge suspected he was the author, Henry excused himself and fled to the safety of home.

Henry Wadsworth Longfellow was born to Stephen and Zilpah Longfellow on February 27, 1807, into an America that was still young. It had been only thirty-one years since the country had declared its independence from England. Thomas Jefferson, the author of that declaration, was now president. Horse-drawn carriages and stagecoaches were used for transportation. Robert Fulton's new invention, the paddle steamboat, had just begun making daily runs from New York to Albany. A true American literature did not yet exist, and no American writer could make a living solely from writing.

Henry spent his boyhood years in the bustling seaport city of Portland in the District of Maine. Maine, not yet a state, was still part of Massachusetts. Portland was almost as old as Boston and had an impressive history of its own. During the Revolution, the British had attacked the town, then called Falmouth, and burned four hundred houses.

Portland was the perfect city for a budding poet. With its busy waterfront where full-rigged ships arrived and departed daily, it was big enough to bring the world to its harbor. Yet, it was small enough that a boy could roam free through its streets and outlying fields. Henry never lost his love for the city of his birth. Throughout his adult life, he returned often to "the beautiful town. . .seated by the sea."

The Wadsworth House, Longfellow's childhood home, was the first brick house built in Portland.

But the poet's story begins much earlier. It begins with Henry's great-great-grandfather, William Longfellow, who immigrated to America from Yorkshire, England, around 1651. He made his living as a blacksmith. His son, Henry's great-grandfather, became a schoolteacher and also served as a clerk of the judicial court in Portland. Henry's grandfather represented Maine in the Massachusetts legislature for many years, finally becoming a judge. Judge Longfellow sent his son, Stephen—Henry's father—to Harvard where he studied law. All of the Longfellow men were practical and ambitious men interested in bettering their lives for themselves and their families. There was no sign of a poet among them.

Henry's mother, Zilpah, could trace her ancestors back to John Alden and Priscilla Mullins, Pilgrims who came to America on the *Mayflower*. Unlike the Longfellows, much of the tradition of the Wadsworth family was military. Ironically, Henry, a pacifist all his life, was named after his mother's brother, who died a hero's death in battle three years before Henry's birth.

And General Peleg Wadsworth, Henry's maternal grandfather, often told Henry about his daring escape from the British after being captured during the Revolutionary War. The general had served as the commander of the whole eastern part of Maine.

When the war ended, the people of Portland elected General Wadsworth to the Massachusetts legislature and later to the Federal Congress. In 1785 he built Wadsworth House, the first brick house in Portland, at what was then the edge of town. Eventually the town grew and surrounded the house, and the old general—who continued to wear the old-fashioned three-cornered hats and knee breeches of Revolutionary days—became restless. He built a new home thirty miles outside Portland in an area that was still frontier. There, he established the town of Hiram. Henry called visits to his grandfather "going into the bush."

When General Wadsworth left Portland, he entrusted the Wadsworth house to his daughter, Zilpah, and her husband, Stephen Longfellow. Zilpah had grown up in the house, and she and Stephen had been married there. They settled into their new home in the fall of 1807 with their children, two-year-old Stephen Jr., and Henry, who was only seven months old.

Stephen and Zilpah Longfellow were highly regarded by the residents of Portland. They were not rich, but they were comfortably well-off. Stephen enjoyed a successful law career and, like his father before him, he represented Maine in the Massachusetts legislature. In 1820 when Maine became a state (an accomplishment in which Stephen played a major role), Portland elected him to Congress.

Stephen Longfellow's law practice, together with his political obligations, required him to spend long stretches of time away from home. Nevertheless, he continued to be a devoted and caring father who made his influence felt. He was not overly strict, but he commanded respect. His children understood that he expected them to follow certain standards. During Stephen's long absences, Zilpah kept him informed about the children's activities through her frequent letters.

Zilpah was an enthusiastic, intelligent woman. She had a deep religious faith, and she appreciated literature and music in a way that her practical husband did not. Zilpah was the parent with whom Henry discussed what book he was reading, and she was undoubtedly the one he trusted to read his first poems. She insisted the children have both dancing and music lessons. Henry learned to play the piano and the flute. When the children grew older, Zilpah encouraged them to invite their friends in for informal sing-a-longs around the piano in the Longfellow parlor.

In this loving and caring household, Henry grew into an affectionate, high-spirited child with a lively imagination. When he was just three years old, he began learning his alphabet from Ma'am Fellows at her small brick schoolhouse on Spring Street.

Then at age five, Henry's parents enrolled him in public school. This was an unusual step because well-to-do families like the Longfellows usually kept their children in private schools. Unfortunately, Henry's new classmates considered him an outsider. Younger than the other children, he did not know how to deal with their sometimes cruel treatment. Soon, his parents removed him from the school and enrolled him in the private school his brother, Stephen, attended. Henry was not a timid child, and he made friends easily, so his difficulty in public school was probably due to his young age.

The Longfellow brothers did well at the small private school, which was just around the corner from their home. And when the owner of the school accepted a headmaster position at the prestigious Portland Academy, he took Henry and Stephen with him.

Henry, six years old by that time, thrived at the academy. His friend and next-door-neighbor, Ned Preble, attended the academy as did a new friend, William Browne, whose family had

Stephen Longfellow, a respected lawyer and politician, expected his children to follow certain standards.

just moved to Portland. Although William was two years ahead of Henry, the two of them became good friends because they shared a mutual interest in writing. They planned elaborate writing projects together. Most of these projects were never carried out, but the shared enthusiasm stimulated Henry to start a notebook and experiment with different forms of writing.

After school and on school holidays, Henry and his brother would meet Ned Preble, and the three would go in search of adventure. The surrounding area was still rural with much open countryside, and the boys could roam over a large area. Some mornings they explored the fields and woods of Munjoy's Hill where Portland residents took the family cow to graze. Other mornings the boys went swimming, splashing, and dunking each other in the sparkling clear water of Back Cove.

Often they went to Deering's Woods, a beautiful grove of oaks on the outskirts of town. To Henry, these woods were a magical place of mysterious shadows and shady nooks. And not far from the woods was a pottery. The boys watched the black-aproned potter sing to himself while he turned shapeless lumps of clay into graceful bowls or vases.

During school vacations, the family often visited either the Wadsworth grandparents in Hiram, or Grandmamma and Grandpa Longfellow at Longfellow Elms in Gorham, fifteen miles from Portland. Many of the country scenes at the Elms—like the blacksmith shop across from Grandpa Longfellow's house—were later celebrated in poems.

When Henry was eight, a fire destroyed the roof of the Portland family home. A storm followed the fire and caused extensive damage to the rooms at the top of the house. Stephen

Longfellow took this opportunity to add a third floor. "We shall have seven very convenient and pleasant chambers [bedrooms]," Stephen wrote Zilpah. They would need the extra space because by 1819, when Henry turned twelve, Stephen and Zilpah had eight children. The Longfellow children remembered their order of birth by chanting:

Stephen and Henry

Elizabeth and Anne

Alex and Mary

Ellen and Sam

During the remodeling of the house, Zilpah, Henry, and Stephen Jr. went to Hiram to visit the Wadsworths. Because Zilpah had not been well, the younger children were sent to stay with their Grandpa and Grandmamma Longfellow in Gorham.

While at Hiram, Henry developed a severe infection in one of his feet. Blood poisoning resulted, and Zilpah wrote her husband that the doctor feared Henry's leg might have to be amputated. But finally after two weeks, the wound began to heal. And Zilpah could write: "There is now no kind of danger of the loss of the leg, and I believe there is none of a stiff ankle." Soon, Henry was well enough to return to Portland and begin another school year.

At the Portland Academy, according to the educational standards of the day, much of Henry's learning was literary. It included studying classic Greek and Roman authors. He also had to master writing Latin before he could be admitted to a college.

Henry's father had graduated from Harvard College in Cambridge, Massachusetts. But like many others who had battled for Maine's admission to the Union, Stephen Longfellow felt an intense loyalty to the new state. Also, old Judge Longfellow, Stephen's father, had been one of the founders of Bowdoin College in Brunswick, Maine, and Stephen himself was now a trustee of the college. Consequently, he chose Bowdoin, which had been modeled after Harvard, for his two oldest sons.

In 1821, at age fourteen, Henry passed the entrance examination for Bowdoin College, as did his older brother, Stephen. However, because Henry was so young, it was decided that both he and his brother would remain at home during their first year of college. This may have been more for Stephen Jr.'s benefit than for Henry's. For despite being older, Stephen, was the less mature of the two. The brothers could continue studying at the academy where they would be tutored in the required freshman subjects.

Henry and his friend, Ned Preble, who would also remain at the academy another year, were eager to see the Bowdoin campus. They took the stagecoach to visit the college, which was thirty miles from Portland. Henry's old friend, William Browne, already a student there, would have showed them around the grounds and introduced them to their new classmates. One of those, George Washington Pierce, became Henry's immediate friend, and they wrote letters back and forth during the school term. Pierce later married Henry's sister, Anne.

Students like Henry, who studied elsewhere during their freshman year, had to be quizzed on freshman subjects before Bowdoin would accept them as sophomores. Henry kept up with the activities of the freshman class at the college through his correspondence with George Pierce. Repeatedly, he questioned George as to what books were being assigned for reading, and he seemed especially anxious to find out if he would be tested in Algebra.

Henry meant to be well-prepared for his debut as a college man when he turned fifteen. And in the fall of 1822—just two years after he had published his first poem and felt the bitter sting of Judge Mellen's criticism—Henry, along with his brother, Stephen, left for Brunswick to begin the sophomore year at Bowdoin College.

Chapter Two

"I Will Be Eminent in Something"

Bowdoin College had been in existence for only twenty years, not a long history for a college. Nevertheless, the quality of its programs and professors rivaled that of Harvard. Bowdoin's enrollment totaled 120 students—all boys. Maine Hall, the campus dormitory, had room for only fifty students. As new arrivals, Henry and Stephen had to find housing off campus. Their father arranged for them to rent rooms from an acquaintance and previous Portland resident, Parson Benjamin Titcomb.

The rooms were furnished as plainly as possible. The cold Maine wind whistled through gaps around the loose-fitting windows, and the only heat came from one small fireplace. No carpets covered the wood floors. Henry wrote immediately to his sisters, asking them to make drapes for the windows and paint some watercolors to brighten up the walls. He also asked them to send lots of gingerbread.

The boys' daily schedule included mandatory attendance at morning chapel. Henry and Stephen rose early and hurried with other student boarders through the darkness down the frozen road to the chapel, where prayers began at 6:00 a.m. After the service, they returned to their lodgings for breakfast. It is little wonder that by December, Henry was longing for the winter vacation break. He wrote his mother: "The long succession of cold days and colder nights—frozen ears—cold feet... all make it dull living in this dreary region of the East. Heigh-ho for the vacation."

A college rule required all students to remain in their rooms during the evening, but college officials found the rule impossible to enforce. Some of the students gathered at local stores or at the popular Ward's tavern, located just outside the college, to play cards and socialize. Stephen participated in these gatherings more frequently than his brother, often neglecting his studies to do so. Henry, loyally, never reported Stephen's behavior to their parents.

Despite some health concerns and admitted homesickness, Henry adjusted well enough to college life. He not only increased the amount of reading he did, but began to sample many different genres of literature. He often wrote his mother about a certain poem or book he was reading.

It was at this time that Henry first showed an interest in the history of Native Americans. After reading about their customs and manners, he wrote indignantly to his mother: "They are a race possessing magnanimity, generosity, benevolence, and pure religion without hypocrisy. . . .They have been most barbarously maltreated by the whites, both in word and deed."

In February, Henry was invited to join the Peucinian Society, a club dedicated to literary pursuits. Few extracurricular activities were available in colleges at that time, and membership in the Peucinian Society offered Henry countless benefits. He forged lasting friendships with students who had similar interests and who encouraged him to write.

The society also made the latest books and the best literary magazines of the day available to its members. Henry discovered American writers that he had never read or even known about. He was more excited by these reading discoveries than by anything he learned in his literature class, which was taught by the president of the college, Rev. William Allen. The president was, by all accounts, a dull teacher and heartily disliked by the students because of his narrow religious views.

In April, toward the end of Henry's sophomore year, an incident occurred that brought the students' discontent out into the open. The newly ordained Rev. Asa Mead conducted a Fast Day service in the chapel, and students were compelled to attend. The boys disliked Rev. Mead because they suspected he was allied with Rev. Allen against some of the newer faculty members, who admitted to supporting more liberal religious beliefs.

William Browne, Henry's old friend from Portland Academy, was completing his senior year at Bowdoin. Browne made the mistake of attending Mead's service under the influence of alcohol. He became ill during the sermon, began vomiting, and had to be led from the chapel by his friends. Immediately, Rev. Mead added a condemnation against drunkenness to his sermon. Annoyed by this, the students began a form of protest called "scraping," which consisted of scuffing their feet on the floor to drown out the speaker.

That evening at prayer service, President Allen reprimanded the students. This angered them further, and when William Browne was expelled and not allowed to graduate, the seniors

Stephen Longfellow Jr. accompanied his younger brother Henry to Bowdoin College.

petitioned for permission to attend Parson Titcomb's church instead of Mead's.

Henry wrote a letter to his father describing what had occurred, followed by an update a few days later:

"All has become quiet again. Yet Mr. Mead seems not to have entirely got over his tantrums. He gave the students a few back-handers the last time he preached—talking a good deal about 'deeds of darkness' to be brought to light here-after and so on. A few of the students have left his meeting: and I also want you to permit me to attend Parson Titcomb's. But I can spend no more time upon a subject so perfectly disgusting to me."

It is clear from Henry's letter that he expected his father to feel as he did. But Stephen Longfellow's immediate reply to his son left no doubt that he thought the action of the students in "scraping" Mr. Mead was highly improper. "I most sincerely hope," he wrote, "that *my sons* have had nothing to do with this unfortunate and disgraceful transaction." Wisely, Henry let the matter drop.

After dividing most of his summer vacation between both sets of grandparents, Henry began his junior year at Bowdoin in October 1823. Once again he and his brother shared a room or "chummed" together. However, an increased enrollment had enabled the college to build a second dormitory, and the brothers could now leave Parson Titcomb's drafty old house and occupy a room on campus. In a letter to his favorite sister, Elizabeth, Henry described with delight the beautiful pine groves visible from his bedroom window.

Henry's junior year was one of personal growth during which he discovered that he wanted to devote his life to literary pursuits. Professor Samuel Phillips Newman, who taught Latin and Greek as well as rhetoric and oratory at Bowdoin, influenced this discovery more than any other person. Newman, recognizing his student's talent, renewed Henry's interest in writing poetry and prose.

Henry had always possessed natural translating skills. But before Professor Newman, he had not understood the creativity involved in translating literature from a foreign language into English. Other instructors had analyzed sentence structure and held vocabulary drills. From Professor Newman, Henry learned that translating another language involved far more than finding the corresponding English words. It meant exploring, discovering and capturing the rhythms and sounds that would convey the beauty and meaning of the work being translated. Several years later, Henry encouraged his sisters to study languages: "I assure you," he said, "that by every language you learn, a new world is opened before you."

During the fall term, Henry began working on a special poem. He planned to enter it in a contest being sponsored by the Boston Shakespeare Jubilee, which was to begin in February 1824. The winning ode would be read at the opening ceremonies.

On January 11, Henry wrote a carefully crafted letter designed to persuade his thrifty father to let him attend the Jubilee during college winter break. He did not mention that he was submitting a poem to the Jubilee. Instead, he pointed out how inexpensive the trip would be because a classmate, who was also making the trip, had invited Henry to share his sleigh. He also reminded his father that he had never been more than fifty miles from Portland. "I am of the opinion," he wrote, "that it is better to know the world from observation than wholly from books. You, who have seen so much of it...will know how this is.... This visit then may...be advantageous as well as agreeable." Henry was allowed to make the trip.

The trip to Boston played its own part in Henry's growing interest in writing. The days were filled with a whirlwind of activities during which Henry and his friends took in the sights of Boston, including the State House, Charlestown, and Harvard. They also attended a private ball where they met some of the most attractive young ladies in Boston. Henry described it as "indeed a most *splendid* entertainment, more so by far than any I had ever beheld before."

Henry's poem did not take the prize in the Jubilee, but that disappointment was eased somewhat by a young woman he met at a friend's home. Carolyn Doane had a sincere interest in modern poetry. She and Henry had long talks during which Henry felt comfortable enough to confide his literary hopes and dreams. Carolyn was sympathetic, and he returned to Boston more determined than ever to continue writing. Henry and Carolyn corresponded for several years.

Not long after returning from Boston, Henry took the first step toward convincing Stephen Longfellow Sr. of the merits of a literary career. He knew that his father wanted him to study law, and if not the law, then medicine or theology. None of these appealed to Henry.

However, out of a deep respect, Henry approached the subject of his future occupation cautiously. On March 13, as he was nearing the end of his junior year, he wrote to his father.

He did not mention his interest in a literary profession. Instead, he began by saying that he had just attended a required medical lecture and continued: "I feel very glad that I am not to be a physician, that there are quite enough in the world without me. And now, as somehow or other the subject has been introduced, I am curious to know what you do intend to make of me! Whether I am to study a profession or not? And if so what profession? I hope your ideas upon this subject will agree with mine, for I have a particular and strong predilection [preference] for one course of life, to which you I fear will not agree. It will not be worth while for me to mention what this is until I become more acquainted with your own wishes."

Stephen Longfellow must have responded, for on April 30 Henry wrote again: "In thinking to make a Lawyer of me, I fear you thought more partially than justly. I do not for my own part think such a coat would suit me. I hardly think Nature designed me for the bar, or the pulpit, or the dissecting room." Careful to soften these remarks, he joked about becoming a farmer.

When Henry returned to Bowdoin in the fall of 1824 for his final year, he remained troubled over his future. He was reluctant to displease his father, but his whole being rebelled at the thought of spending his life in any of the "accepted" professions. He shared his feelings with his cousin, George Wells. "I cannot make a lawyer of any eminence," he wrote, "because I have not a talent for argument; I am not good enough for a minister—and as to Physic [Medicine], I utterly and absolutely detest it."

By early December Henry could bear the uncertainty no longer. He wrote again to his father. Abandoning his previous indirect approach, he spoke from the heart: "I wish to know fully your inclination with regard to the profession I am to pursue, when I leave college. . . . I have already hinted to you what would best please me. I want to spend one year at Cambridge [Harvard] for the purpose of reading History, and of becoming familiar with the best authors in . . . literature. . . . After leaving Cambridge I would attach myself to some literary periodical publication, by which I could maintain myself. The fact is . . . I most eagerly aspire after future eminence in literature, my whole soul burns most ardently for it, and every earthly thought centers in it. . . ."

In this same letter, Henry wrote that after sending three poems to a new magazine called the *U.S. Literary Gazette*, the editor, Theophilus Parsons, had asked him to become a regular contributor. Since the *Gazette* also published the poems of William Cullen Bryant, America's most respected poet of the day, Henry was justifiably proud.

Henry basked in Parsons' praise that "your literary talents are of no ordinary character." Parsons, who usually paid only for prose, was impressed enough to offer money for the poems. For his three poems, Henry received $17 minus the *Gazette's* $3 subscription price.

After writing his father, Henry waited anxiously for a reply. Weeks went by and none came. The silence itself seemed to give the answer. Finally, on December 31, Henry made one final plea. Hoping to appeal to his father's practical nature, he pointed out that even if he had to enter one of the professions, the year at Harvard would be useful preparation. "Whatever I do study ought to be engaged in with all my soul," he told his father, "for

Bowdoin College had only been in existence twenty years when Henry and his older brother Stephhen enrolled in 1822.

I *will be eminent* in something." He reasoned that if he did not succeed in the literary world, there would still be time to study for a profession.

At last the long awaited letter arrived. Stephen Longfellow was not unsympathetic to his son's dreams. However, as a parent, he wanted to ensure that Henry could support himself comfortably in the future. He wrote:

"A literary life, to one who has the means of support, must be very pleasant. But there is not wealth enough in this country to afford encouragement and patronage to merely literary men. And as you have not had the fortune . . . to be born rich, you must adopt a profession which will afford you subsistence. . . . With regard to your spending a year at Cambridge, I have always thought it might be beneficial; and if my. . . finances. . . allow, I [shall] be very happy to gratify you. . . ."

Stephen Longfellow Sr. had been slow in answering Henry's letters because he was occupied with more pressing concerns. In December, Stephen Jr. had been expelled from Bowdoin for poor conduct that included "introducing spirituous liquors into the college." Young Stephen ultimately returned to Bowdoin and graduated with his class, but his conduct had caused his father much anxiety.

Meanwhile, Henry was overjoyed that he was to be allowed the year at Harvard. He wrote his father that at the end of that time, he would respect his wishes and enter the law. But despite this seeming acceptance, Henry had not let go of his dream. Several months after receiving his father's letter, he wrote Parsons, the *Literary Gazette* editor, asking if the *Gazette* might have an opening for him as an assistant editor after he graduated.

Parsons' response was crushing. In essence, he repeated Stephen Longfellow Sr.'s argument that no one could make a living through writing alone. Parsons, however, was not as kind. "Get through your present delusion as soon as you can," he wrote, "& then you will see how wise it will be for you to devote yourself to the law."

Three weeks later, Henry received his diploma from Bowdoin. In 1825, the graduation ceremony was not held until after summer vacation. Henry—who had graduated fourth in his class of 38—was one of four students chosen to speak at the commencement program on September 7. He was assigned the topic of "Our Native Writers." In his seven-minute oration, he spoke passionately about the need to encourage native writers if America was ever to have a national literature.

Among those seated in the audience was the Honorable Benjamin Orr, a trustee of Bowdoin. He had evaluated Henry's senior final examination, which had included a translation from the classical Roman poet, Horace. Orr had been so impressed by the translation that he had made special inquiries about Henry. Now as he listened to the young graduate pour out his feelings, Orr made a decision that would change Longfellow's life forever.

Chapter Three

"I Have Reached the Shores of the Old World"

After the graduation ceremonies ended, the Bowdoin trustees held a meeting. They voted first to establish a department of modern languages that would teach French, Spanish, and Italian. Then they turned to the more difficult problem of finding a qualified professor. Because only three other colleges in the country had a modern language department, it would be impossible to find a professor experienced in teaching those languages.

Professor Benjamin Orr recommended Henry for the new professorship. He was not yet qualified for such a position, and Orr and the other trustees acknowledged that. But they also knew Henry's scholastic record, and they were familiar with his published work. They voted to offer Henry the professorship on condition that he study in Europe for two years—at his own expense—in order to learn the necessary languages.

This amazing turn of events must have seemed miraculous to eighteen-year-old Henry. Not only was he freed from the specter of studying law, but two years in Europe stretched out before him like the ribbons on a surprise birthday gift. Henry was eager to leave, but he would have to wait until spring because ocean travel was dangerous during the fall and winter. At his father's insistence, he studied law while he waited for spring.

In April 1826, a month before his ship was due to sail from New York, Henry left his Portland home. "I feel," his mother told him, "as if you were going into a thousand perils." Yet, she encouraged him in his "pursuit of knowledge."

Henry stopped in Boston to visit friends and relatives and, as was the custom, to obtain letters of introduction to notable people abroad. George Ticknor, the professor of modern languages at Harvard, invited him to dinner. Ticknor gave him several introductory letters, including one to Washington Irving, who was traveling in Europe. Irving's *Sketch Book* had been Henry's favorite schoolboy book.

By May 14, Henry had arrived in New York. He wrote to his sister, Anne: "I sail for Le Havre de Grace [in France] tomorrow . . . on board the Ship Cadmus . . . . There are twenty cabin passengers, two of which are ladies—and many of the gentlemen are French, which will be of great advantage to me. The ship is a very fine one and the Capt. has the reputation of being an excellent man. I . . . anticipate a good passage."

On Monday morning, May 15, 1826, Henry boarded the *Cadmus*, bound for Europe. Now nineteen years old and a professor-elect of modern languages—languages he did not yet know—Henry was on his own.

Exactly one month later, Henry wrote his mother that he had "reached the shores of the Old World." Later he would write:

"To my youthful imagination the Old World was a kind of Holy Land, lying afar off beyond the blue horizon of the ocean; and when its shores first rose upon my sight, looming through the hazy atmosphere of the sea, my heart swelled with the deep emotion of the pilgrim, when he sees afar the spire which rises above the shrine of his devotion."

On June 19, Henry arrived in Paris by stagecoach. A cousin, who was studying medicine in Paris, had rented a room for him. The boarding house was within five minutes walking distance of the principal lecture rooms and colleges. Henry attended university lectures, but did not enroll in formal classes—a practice he would follow in all of the countries he visited. He preferred to mingle with the people so that he learned their culture, as well as their language.

In 1826, the transatlantic mail system was erratic. Often, months went by between letters from home, and Henry was forced to make decisions on his own. He could not wait for instructions from his father. Letters to his family reflected Henry's inexperience with making independent decisions. Each letter seemed to outline a new plan, and his parents were frequently left wondering what he had decided. Although homesick at times, Henry sounded cheerful when he wrote his brother, Stephen, in July: "After five weeks' residence in Paris I have settled down in something half-way between a Frenchman and a New Englander . . . . That is to say, I have good home-feelings at heart—but have decorated my outward man with a long-waisted thin coat—claret-coloured—and a pair of linen pantaloons:—and on Sundays and other [festival] days—I appear in all the glory of a little hard French hat—glossy—and brushed—and rolled up at the sides . . . . In this garb I jostle along amongst the crowds. . . ."

This description of Parisian finery drew a rebuke from Henry's father, who reminded him sternly to "remember that you are an American, and . . . you should retain your own National Costume. You will find it much more convenient and less expensive." In a subsequent letter, Henry told his father he had been joking.

By October, Stephen Longfellow Sr. had begun to worry that life in Paris may have diverted his young son from his purpose. He wrote that he had expected that, by now, Henry would have become competent enough in the French language that he could move on to Spain. He also mentioned that his son's expenses had been more than expected. "You are," his father cautioned, "surrounded with temptations and allurements and it will be necessary for you to set a double guard upon yourself. . . ."

Henry was stung by his father's letter. "You . . . over-rate my abilities. . . ," he wrote back, "if you think that I am already master of the French. . . . I had no idea. . .that it was indeed so difficult to learn a language." He admitted the temptations around him were plentiful, but said he, himself, did not have the time to partake of them.

"The truth is," Henry continued, "that the heavy responsibility which I have taken upon myself . . . together with the continual solicitude [concern] about the final result of my studies, and the fear that you will be displeased with my expenses—are hanging with a terrible weight upon me."

Only one day after writing this letter, Henry escaped from the pressures by embarking on a ten-day walking tour. He rambled through towns and villages, soaking up the scenes and pleasures of the French countryside, as he had always dreamed of doing.

Henry did not attempt to hide his truancy. On the contrary, in a long letter to his brother Stephen he described the entire adventure. Mischievously, he told his brother about joining a group of travelers that included several young girls, "in order, you know—to study character."

By November, Henry was back in Paris. He knew better than to try justifying his behavior to his father. Instead, he wrote his mother. He explained that he had been tempted to run away from his studies, because he feared he would never have another opportunity to see that part of France. He defended himself by pointing out that he had spoken only French for the entire ten days, and that he had actually saved money because he had traveled very economically.

Three months later, Henry wrote his father that he was "well satisfied" with his knowledge of the French language, and that he planned to leave Paris for Spain. Although he spoke kindly of the French people, he was not sorry to leave Paris, and told his family that he looked forward to a happier life in Spain.

Traveling through mountainous country as he left France, Longfellow caught glimpses of the sea. "It was the first time I had seen it for nearly a twelve-month," he told his father. "I was glad to hear its old familiar voice. I thought I was quite near you again. It seemed but a step—a little step—from one shore to the other."

Despite dire warnings from the French that bandits made it dangerous to travel to Spain, Henry arrived safely in Madrid on

March 9, 1827. He fell in love with Spain and its people, whom he found warmer and kinder than the French.

Henry wrote to his sister Elizabeth describing the courtly manners of the Spanish: "In saluting a lady—the common phrase is, 'Senora, I throw myself at your grace's feet!' The lady replies—'I kiss your grace's hand, Senor!' How would that do in Portland?" And he thought the Basque girls enchanting. "They have most beautiful dark eyes—fine teeth—a sun-burnt complexion—and glossy black hair down to the knees in a large beautiful braid."

Nothing about Spain disappointed Henry. He met Washington Irving there, and even his idol lived up to expectations. Although Henry mingled at times with the cream of Spain's society, he preferred traveling through the countryside. He joined in the merriment at village festivals, even learning the dances. After one such excursion, he wrote in his journal: "I have seen a little of Spanish rural life & am much delighted with it. I like to see things in reality—not in painting—to study men—not books."

Henry stayed in Spain for eight months, and it never lost its fascination for him. But although he made three more trips to Europe in later years, he never returned to Spain. Perhaps he feared he would find it changed, or find himself changed from the romantic youth who had danced with the village peasants. Later, he wrote a poem titled "Castles In Spain," which began: "How much of my young heart, O Spain/Went out to thee in days of yore!"

In late November of 1827, Henry sailed for Genoa, Italy. One of his fellow travelers was George Greene, the grandson of

General Nathanael Greene, a hero of the American Revolution. There was an instant affinity between the two men that developed into a lifelong friendship. Throughout his life, Henry would share personal confidences with George Greene that he shared with no other friends.

When Henry arrived in Italy, he had been away from home for over a year and a half. He wrote his mother that he was homesick for Spain, but he may have been homesick for Portland, because he added: "Next to going home—let me go to Spain."

However, Henry remained in Italy for over a year, spending most of that time in Rome. He took side trips to Pisa, Florence, Naples, and Venice, but always returned to Rome. In long letters home, Henry assured his parents that he was keeping up with his studies, but he also described the carnivals and fancy balls he attended.

Stephen Longfellow Sr., reading between the lines of Henry's letters and noting his son's seeming inability to stay away from Rome, began to suspect a possible romantic involvement. Henry, himself, was careful not to mention any such entanglement, if one existed.

However, in mid-September 1828, Henry broke free from Rome. He was traveling through Italy, en route to Germany, when he received a disturbing letter from his father. Stephen Longfellow wrote that the Bowdoin trustees had voted to offer Henry a position as an instructor instead of as a professor. An instructorship paid much less and did not carry the prestige of a professorship. The news dealt a devastating blow to Henry's pride.

Henry was especially angry that the board had decided he was too young. "Were they not aware of this three years ago?" he wrote his father. He went on to say that he would not accept such a position and bravely insisted that he had no anxiety about his future. He boasted that he could now speak and write French and Spanish as fluently as English. He could read Portugese, and his Italian was so good that Italians did not realize he was American until he told them.

Displaying his developing independence, Henry continued his letter: "Do you, then, advise [me] to accept of such a situation as is proffered me? No, I think you cannot . . . . I beg of you not to think that this [refusal] springs from any undue degree of arrogance . . . but I must assert a freedom of thought and of speech."

By February 1829, Henry was in Gottingen, Germany, where he reunited with his childhood friend, Ned Preble. Seeing his old friend lifted his spirits. On February 27, his twenty-second birthday, he cheerfully wrote his father he was confident that by the end of summer "my friends can probably think of some other situation equally good for me as a professorship at Brunswick."

However, the loss of the professorship had jolted Henry. As a result, he took a more serious attitude toward his studies in Germany than he had in any other country. He attended lectures at the university as usual, but he also hired an academic tutor to help him learn German.

Late in March, Henry wrote his sister Elizabeth that everyone else was on vacation, but he remained "entrenched behind a rampart of books." In this same letter, he congratulated Elizabeth on her recent engagement to be married and regretted that he could not write a poem for her worthy of the event. "My poetic career is finished," he told her. "Since I left America, I have hardly put two lines together."

Shortly after Henry wrote this letter, Elizabeth became ill. He wrote his mother in May that he was hoping for his sister's recovery. But in June a letter from his father urged him to return home immediately because Elizabeth was gravely ill.

Henry left Germany at once. But while he waited in Paris to begin his voyage home, he received the news that Elizabeth had died. This loss of a favored sister marked his first close encounter with death. In a sense, it completed, as well, his passage from boyhood to manhood.

By August 27, 1829, Longfellow was back in Portland. He immediately wrote to the trustees at Bowdoin College, thanking them for electing him instructor of modern languages, but adding: "I am sorry that . . . I cannot accept the appointment. The Professorship . . . with a salary equal to that of the other Professors would certainly not have been refused. But having at great expense, devoted four years to the acquisition of the French, Spanish, Italian, and German languages, I cannot accept a subordinate station with a salary so disproportionate to the duties required."

In less than a week, the Bowdoin trustees responded. They offered Longfellow the title of professor with a compromise salary of $800, which was more than an instructor received, but less than the $1,000 a year paid to professors. However, they appointed him to serve as college librarian at an additional salary of $100. Longfellow accepted with the understanding that in the future his salary would be made equal to that of the other professors.

Longfellow now prepared to enter a new phase of his life. He had left Maine a boy. He had returned a man. But with images of castles on the Rhine, lofty cathedrals in Rome, carnivals and fiestas in Spain and the flashing dark eyes of Basque maidens whirling through his mind, was he ready to settle down at a small, provincial college in Brunswick, Maine?

Chapter Four

"Good Fortune" and "Sorrow Unspeakable"

No one had asked Longfellow if he wanted to teach. And in his eagerness to escape studying law, it is doubtful whether he even asked himself. He would always have a love-hate relationship with teaching, alternately enjoying and resenting it.

However, he approached his first year with high expectations and a dedication that left no room for writing poetry. In his five years of teaching at Bowdoin, he wrote only two or three poems, and those were special-occasion poems written by request. For the most part, his writing was limited to scholarly articles and textbooks.

Longfellow was twenty-two years old when he walked onto Bowdoin campus as a professor. He was not only the head of the new department of Modern Languages, he *was* the department. That first year, he taught only French and Spanish, but the following year he would add classes in German and Italian.

Since the college provided few textbooks for these classes, Longfellow immediately began translating and adapting an elementary French grammar for use by his students. This French grammar, like his later Spanish and Italian grammars, was printed at his own expense with the reluctant financial help of his father.

The attractive young professor was immediately popular with his students. Longfellow had, after all, been one of them only a few years earlier. He had a fondness for colorful clothes, and he was not as rigid in his views as the older professors were. Because of his foreign travels, an aura of the exotic surrounded him. Students sought out his classes.

Nevertheless, Longfellow found it difficult after his European travels to adjust to the small-town atmosphere of Bowdoin. He was lonely because he had little in common with the people he met, including the other professors. "Buried in the dust and cobwebs of this country college," he soon wrote to a friend, "moth and rust begin to consume me. I am *with* them but not *of* them, may I truly say of those around me."

His loneliness only increased when he learned in the spring that George Greene, the friend he had met in Italy, had brought home an Italian bride. By summer, however, Longfellow was involved in his own courtship.

Longfellow met Mary Storer Potter while on a visit to Portland. Mary's father, the formidable Judge Barrett Potter, was a widower who guarded his three daughters with a fierceness designed to instill fear into the hearts of all suitors. At first Longfellow's sister Anne smuggled his letters to Mary.

On July 13, 1830, after Mary had sent him a ticket to a Portland ball, Longfellow enclosed his reply in a letter to Anne. He told his sister, "I fancy that if the Judge finds out that I have written a letter to his daughter, he will stand on the defensive. So please hand it to her ladyship when no one is nigh. . . ."

But soon Longfellow was courting Mary openly, and by the end of September he wrote Judge Potter to thank him for "placing in my hands the happiness of a daughter." The marriage would take place a year later.

Meanwhile, Longfellow began his second year of teaching. And he started writing scholarly articles for the *North American Review*. Alexander Everett, the *Review* editor, suggested he also write for the *New-England Magazine*, a new literary periodical. Longfellow wrote articles about his European travels for the new magazine—articles that would eventually form the beginning of his first non-scholarly book. He found such pleasure in writing these less formal articles that he began to grow dissatisfied with his teaching duties. They left him little free time for such pursuits.

As Longfellow's third year of teaching approached, he poured out his growing resentment to his sister Anne in a letter written three weeks before his marriage. "I have aimed higher than this;" he wrote, "and I cannot believe that all my aspirations are to terminate in the drudgery of a situation, which gives me no opportunity to distinguish myself."

Longfellow and "Little Mary," as he called her, were married on September 14, 1831, at the Potter home in Portland. Longfellow was twenty-four and Mary was nineteen.

Mary Potter Longfellow, petite and pale-skinned, attractive and well educated but never in robust health and not an energetic woman, nevertheless took a great interest in her husband's work and filled the role of a professor's wife well. The first year of their marriage they lived in a boarding house, because Longfellow had been unable to find a suitable house he could afford.

Mary Storer Potter Longfellow

Married life brought Longfellow a measure of contentment. He traveled with Mary to Boston to consult editors at Colonel Metcalf's University Press, where his grammar books were being printed. There he met Charles Folsom.

Folsom had been a tutor and librarian at Harvard College before resigning to take an editorial position at University Press. He introduced Longfellow to influential people at Harvard. Longfellow found these people stimulating, and he returned to Bowdoin determined to write something other than textbooks. He wrote to Folsom, who was editing his grammar books and who was quickly becoming a close friend: "I mean to turn author and write a book—not a *grammar.*"

In a letter to George Greene, Longfellow shared his excitement about a possible book: "I am writing a book—a kind of Sketch-Book of France, Spain, Germany, and Italy;—composed of descriptions—sketches of character—tales illustrating manners and customs. . . . Whether the book will ever see the light is yet uncertain. . . . I find that it requires little courage to publish grammars and school-books—but in the department of fine writing, or attempts at fine writing—it requires vastly more courage."

Longfellow titled the book *Outre-Mer: A Pilgrimage Beyond the Sea.* It was to be published in two parts. In July of 1833 he wrote Greene that he had mailed him "the first [part] of "Outre-Mer."

Meanwhile, Longfellow's unhappiness at Brunswick continued to build. Even as a student at Bowdoin, he had disliked the politics of college government. As a Unitarian who rejected many of the basic teachings of the Puritans who had founded

New England, his religious views did not conform to Bowdoin's rigid beliefs. And when a religious revivalism overwhelmed the campus in the spring of 1834, Longfellow voiced his disgust with the resulting hysteria. This angered the citizens of Brunswick.

Mary Longfellow wrote to her husband's sisters: "The students are so much excited that they cannot attend to their studies, and Pres't [President Allen] and most of the Professors are in the same state. . . . There is not a single house in town that has not been visited by some of [the revivalists], excepting [ours]. I believe they think we are among the doomed . . . . At the meeting of the Fire Company Dr. Lincoln motioned that if Prof. Longfellow's house should burn down no one should move to put it out. . . . No one would second [the motion]. . . . In these exciting times you must not be surprised to hear that our house is set on fire. . . ."

The Longfellows' house was not burned, but Longfellow soon became as desperate to escape from Bowdoin as he had once been to escape studying law. He sought other teaching positions, pursued government posts, and even considered establishing a women's college. One plan after another failed to materialize, including the final one, which was to edit his own magazine.

But fate and Longfellow's growing number of friends in Cambridge, thanks in part to Charles Folsom's introductions, were about to take a hand. These friends had been working behind the scenes at Harvard to find a place for Longfellow on the Harvard staff. Learning that Professor Ticknor planned to retire, they wrote letters to Josiah Quincy, Harvard's president, suggesting Longfellow as Ticknor's replacement. And Ticknor, who had recognized Longfellow's potential the first time they met, was pleased to recommend him.

On December 1, 1834, Longfellow's long-sought liberation from Bowdoin arrived in the mail. A letter from President Quincy invited Longfellow to replace Professor Ticknor as Harvard's professor of modern languages. The salary would be $1,500 per year. If Longfellow wanted to spend a year or two in Europe at his own expense, Ticknor would continue in the position until Longfellow returned.

"So here it comes at last," Longfellow wrote in his journal. He sent a copy of Quincy's letter to his father and wrote: "Good fortune comes at last; and I certainly shall not reject it."

Longfellow's father argued against his son making a second trip to Europe, because he did not want him to increase his debts. And Mary Longfellow, who had no desire to travel abroad, tried to persuade her husband not to make the trip. But Longfellow was determined to go. The opportunity to perfect his German was his official reason for going, but the trip also offered a respite from teaching. Although Harvard would be much more pleasing to Longfellow than Bowdoin, he would always chafe under the "yoke" of teaching.

In February, he accepted the position at Harvard and resigned from Bowdoin. On March 21, he wrote George Greene: "We go [to Europe] in a company of four; two Boston ladies Miss Goddard and Miss. Crowinshield having joined our party. This will . . . leave me more leisure than if Mary went alone . . . for the ladies will amuse each other, without too much of my assistance. This is a very uncivil speech for me to make; but as

I go for the purpose of studying, I shall want as much of the time to myself as possible."

They sailed from New York harbor on April 10, 1835 and arrived in London on May 8.

Longfellow wanted to study the Scandinavian languages. After a month, he and his companions left London for Stockholm, Sweden. They stayed in Stockholm for two months while Longfellow studied with a professor from the university. "I am slowly picking up crumbs in the Swedish language. . . . It comes," he wrote, "word by word, and phrase by phrase."

But the two months in Stockholm were not pleasant ones. Mary Longfellow, who was pregnant, had not been well since leaving England. To make matters worse, the weather was extremely cold, and it rained every day of their stay.

From Stockholm, they went to Copenhagen where Longfellow studied Danish, tutored by a scholar on the staff of the Royal Library. At Copenhagen, the four travelers dropped to three when Miss Goddard was summoned home because her father was ill.

Meanwhile, Mary Longfellow's condition did not improve. Amsterdam was their next scheduled stop, and out of concern for Mary, Longfellow decided they should travel from Copenhagen to Amsterdam by boat, rather than by carriage as they had planned.

Despite this precaution, Mary suffered a miscarriage in Amsterdam and came close to dying. But after three weeks, she had improved and felt well enough to travel to Rotterdam. To preserve Mary's strength, they took three days to make the short journey. Nevertheless, she experienced a relapse at the end of the trip.

Longfellow thought all Mary needed was prolonged bed rest. He never doubted that she would recover. He hired an English-speaking nurse, and together with Mary's traveling companion, Clara Crowinshield, kept a constant vigil at his wife's bedside. But Mary grew weaker and weaker.

Finally, on November 24, Longfellow accepted how ill Mary was. He wrote in his journal, "My poor Mary is worse to-day. Sinking—sinking. My heart is heavy; yet I still hope. . . ." And on the morning of November 29, 1835, he wrote: "This morning between one and two o'clock, my Mary—my beloved Mary—ceased to breathe."

Longfellow was overcome not only with grief, but also with guilt. He could not forget that Mary had not wanted to come to Europe. Over and over, he asked himself if this was what had come of his ambition to be "eminent?"

Still numb from the shock, Longfellow did the things that had to be done. He wrote Mary's father, and he arranged for his wife's body to be shipped to America. It would accomplish nothing for him to accompany the body home, but he could not bear to remain in Rotterdam where Mary had died.

Longfellow continued on to Heidelberg and spent the winter there as had been previously planned. But he had great difficulty concentrating on work. "I cannot study," he wrote in his journal two months later. "All day I am weary and sad—and at night I cry myself to sleep like a child. Not a page can I read without my thoughts wandering from it."

To add to his distress, Longfellow received news from home

This portrait of Fanny (right) and Mary Appleton was painted in 1836.

that his friend and brother-in-law, George Washington Pierce, had died fourteen days before Mary. Longfellow plodded on through the winter. He forced himself to attend lectures and study the German language and literature as much as possible. Much of his future poetry, especially his ballads, would show the influence of German legends.

With the coming of spring, Longfellow found it impossible to continue studying. He considered returning home, but decided to first visit his friend George Greene, who was living in Italy. On the way, he would tour Austria and Switzerland.

Travel did not make Longfellow forget his grief. "Traveling," he wrote, "is not always a cure for sadness." But as so often happened in Longfellow's life, fate took a hand. For in Switzerland he met Nathan Appleton, a prosperous merchant from Boston, who was traveling with his family.

Nathan Appleton had two talented and beautiful daughters. The younger daughter, Frances, who was called Fanny, was a lively young woman, only seventeen, with dark flashing eyes that reminded Longfellow of the Basque maidens he had admired in Spain. "There was not one discordant thing in her;" he wrote later, "but a perfect harmony of figure, and face, and soul. . . . And he who had a soul. . .must of necessity love her, and, having once loved her, could love no other woman forevermore."

Longfellow enjoyed the entire Appleton family, and when he was invited to join them in a week of travel, he accepted gratefully. He spent long hours swimming with Fanny's brother, Tom. He escorted Fanny and her sister, Mary, around the towns. On August 2, he wrote in his diary that he had walked with Miss Fanny after dinner. "It was delightful," he added. "Since I have joined [this family]. . .the time passes pleasantly. I now for the first time enjoy Switzerland."

Longfellow was jolted back to earth when he received a letter from Clara Crowinshield (still in Heidelberg) that she wanted to go home. Reminded of his chaperone responsibilities, he returned immediately to Heidelberg and made preparations for returning to America.

And back in Switzerland, Fanny Appleton wrote in her diary: "Miss Mr. L. considerably."

Chapter Five

"Voices of the Night"

Longfellow arrived at Harvard University in December 1836. Cambridge, Massachusetts, with its narrow, winding streets and small houses crammed close together was then referred to as "The Village." Pigs were still kept in sties behind the college. Harvard, itself, was small, having approximately 400 students, most of them local residents.

But Cambridge overflowed with new ideas, and with poets and novelists and orators who offered Longfellow the intellectual stimulation he craved. Boston was within easy walking distance or could be reached via the horse-drawn bus. There, one could see the latest stage plays and hear public lectures on science and literature by people like Ralph Waldo Emerson.

And over on Boston's fashionable Beacon Street, Nathan Appleton's splendid home awaited the return of its occupants.

The Appleton family would be traveling in Europe for another year. Longfellow waited impatiently for their return. He later referred to that year as "a whole year's delirium of hope."

When he had met Fanny Appleton in Switzerland, the time had not been appropriate for a serious romance. Longfellow's wife had been dead only six months, and Fanny, ten years younger than Longfellow, was more interested in a flirtation than in a major romance. Nevertheless, it had been love at first sight for Longfellow, and he was confident Fanny had felt the same attraction.

That confidence is apparent in Longfellow's first letter to Fanny, written shortly after he arrived at Harvard. On their walks together in Switzerland, he had helped her with her German. Building on that shared memory, he enclosed a translation of a German poem "as a kind of Valentine."

The poem, Longfellow told her, will "serve. . .as a German lesson, during the master's absence. He hopes to resume hereafter his instructions. . . ." By the "master," he clearly meant himself. Longfellow had made a mistake. Fanny would understand that he spoke of more than German lessons, and she would not appreciate his presumptuous familiarity after such a short acquaintance.

Unaware of his blunder, Longfellow happily settled in at Harvard. He already had friends there, among them Cornelius Felton, the professor of Greek. Felton introduced him to three other young men: Henry Cleveland, a former proctor at Harvard; George Hilliard, a young lawyer; and Hilliard's law partner, Charles Sumner, who lectured at Harvard's law school.

The five men, all with a common interest in literature, became such good friends that they started an informal group called "The Five of Clubs." They were all under thirty, and except for Hilliard, all unmarried. At Saturday dinners they debated topics of the day, told tall stories, played whist [a card game], and read and critiqued each other's manuscripts. Later, when they had pieces published, they reviewed each other's work with such praise that newspapers mockingly called them "The Mutual Admiration Society."

Within this group, it was Charles Sumner who became Longfellow's dearest friend. A strong bond developed between these two very different men that lasted throughout their lives. Longfellow's home always provided a haven for Sumner, both in the early years and later when Sumner became an avid antislavery advocate and was elected to the United States Senate.

At last, Longfellow felt content. He enjoyed the camaraderie with his friends, and he was pleased with his duties at the college. He did not teach classes his first term, because French, Spanish, Italian, and German were being taught by the foreign instructors who had served on Professor Ticknor's staff.

Longfellow was asked only to prepare a course of lectures on European literature for the spring term. These lectures were highly popular with the students, because unlike most of the professors, Longfellow did not write out lectures and read them. Instead, he lectured from notes, making his presentations seem more like friendly discussions.

During this spring term, Longfellow received a letter from Nathaniel Hawthorne, a former classmate at Bowdoin. Hawthorne enclosed his just-published book, *Twice-Told Tales*. He did not ask Longfellow to review it, though he admitted later that was what he had hoped would happen. Longfellow not only reviewed the book, he praised it as coming "from the hand of a man of genius." They had not known each other well in

Anti-slavery politician Charles Sumner became Longfellow's life-long friend.

college, and this marked the beginning of a friendship between the two authors.

Throughout the spring semester, Longfellow lived in the boarding house where Felton lived. But before the fall term began, he sought rooms at the historic Craigie House where George Washington had lived while the British had Boston under siege.

Mrs. Craigie was at first reluctant to rent to Longfellow because she thought he was a student. She also doubted if he was a "real gentleman" because of the colorful clothes he wore. But when she found out he was the author of *Outre Mer*, which she had read, she changed her mind and rented Longfellow two large, comfortable rooms on the third floor.

Longfellow was enchanted by the elegance of Craigie House and its beautiful gardens. By the start of the fall term, he had settled into the house where he was destined to live the rest of his life.

Autumn of 1837 promised to be a golden time for Longfellow. He began the fall semester at Harvard with enthusiasm—lecturing on the German poet Goethe. And September brought the return of the Appletons.

By October, Longfellow was courting Fanny Appleton. He sent flowers accompanied by poems written especially for her, and he frequently walked to Boston to call at her home. It is probable that Longfellow impulsively proposed marriage soon after Fanny returned. At the very least, he confessed his love for her. In either case, she rejected him. In the nineteenth century, and especially in the rarefied air of Beacon Street society, a gentleman did not rush affairs of the heart.

On January 6, 1838, Longfellow poured out his grief and disappointment in a letter to George Greene: "I have no merriment in my life. A leaden melancholy hangs over me . . . .To tell you the whole truth—I saw in Switzerland and travelled with a fair lady—whom I now love passionately. . .and have loved since I knew her. A glorious and beautiful being—young—and a woman *not* of talent but of *genius!*—indeed a most rare, sweet woman whose name is Fanny Appleton. . . . She lends no favorable ear to my passion and for my love gives me only friendship. Good friends we are—but she says she loves me not. Among all my friends you are the *only* one, who can *understand*. . .this point. I shall win this lady, or I shall die."

Socially, it was almost impossible for Longfellow to avoid meeting the Appleton sisters. And in any case, he treasured these chance encounters even though he felt worse afterwards. Also, because he maintained his friendship with Fanny's sister and brother, Longfellow continued to visit the Appleton home. Fanny Appleton was always gracious and polite, but remained coolly indifferent.

This rejection, combined with the losses Longfellow had previously suffered, brought a new maturity that deepened and enriched him. He began to write poetry again. On July 26, 1838, he sat down at his open window and wrote "Psalm of Life," the poem that would bring him his first fame. He said later that he was unwilling at first to show anyone the poem, "the poem being a voice from my inmost heart at a time when I was rallying from depression."

On October 22, 1838, Longfellow wrote to Greene that the "'Dark Ladie,'" [Fanny Appleton] showed no signs of yielding.

And in November—partly in an effort to continue courting Fanny Appleton in a roundabout way—he began work on a novel he called *Hyperion*. It was a thinly disguised story of his meeting with Fanny in Switzerland, and his subsequent heartbreak.

In August 1839, one week before the book came out, Longfellow wrote to Greene: "I have not got over it. I am as much in love as ever. Depend upon it my dear George, there are two mighty wills at work here. . . . The lady says she *will not*! I say she *shall*!" He went on to explain that the heroine of *Hyperion* was modeled after Fanny, but hastened to add that "there is no betrayal of confidence . . . and the lady [is] so painted . . . as to make her fall in love with her own sweet image in the book."

But Fanny's reaction to the book was not what Longfellow had expected. Instead, she was embarrassed and humiliated. The book was the hot topic of gossip in Boston, and everyone knew that Paul Flemming and Mary Ashburton—the hero and heroine of the novel—represented Longfellow and Fanny Appleton. Shortly after he sent her a copy of the book, they met accidentally on Boston Common. She looked the other way and passed without speaking.

Fanny wrote to one of her cousins who was an aspiring writer: "Don't make me [the subject] of any of your 'thought children,' as you call 'em. I . . . have already been hoisted into such a public notoriety by a certain impertinent friend of mine . . . that I am entirely disgusted with the honor. . . ."

Although Longfellow did not share his feelings for Fanny Appleton with his family, he kept in close touch with them about other matters. He wrote often—especially to his father—and frequently visited Portland. A month after *Hyperion* was published, he wrote his father that he was planning to publish soon a volume of poetry.

That book, *Voices of the Night,* was published in December 1839 and was an immediate success. The same critics who had denounced Longfellow's novel had only praise for his poems. Two weeks after its publication, he wrote his father: "You do not know how grandly my *Voices* has succeeded. The publisher tells me he has only forty copies left . . . out of nine hundred printed."

But Fanny Appleton, still angry, wrote scornfully to her cousin: "The Prof has collected his vagrant poems into a neat little volume christened mournfully *Voices of the Night.* He does not look like a night-bird and is more of a mocking-bird than a nightingale, though he has some sweetly plaintive notes."

Inspired by the success of *Voices*, Longfellow composed poems at an increasingly rapid pace. He wrote in his journal on December 30:

"I sat by my fire. . .when suddenly it came into my mind to write the 'Ballad of the Schooner Hesperus;' which I accordingly did. . . . I feel pleased with the ballad. It hardly cost me an effort. It did not come into my mind by lines, but by stanzas.

Writing to George Greene a few days later in the new year, Longfellow said he planned to write more ballads. "The *natural ballad*," he wrote, "is a virgin soil here in New England; and there are great materials."

The next two years were productive ones. In 1840, Longfellow sold "The Wreck of the Hesperus" for twenty-five dollars. (Many of his poems were sold first to magazines before they were collected into a book.) And by the end of the year he wrote his father that *Voices of the Night* had gone into its third edition, and "the fourth is now printing."

Longfellow continued writing poems at an almost frantic pace. "At present, my dear friend," he wrote to Sam Ward, "my soul is wrapped up in poetry." Ward, whom he had met on his second trip to Europe, had not only become a close friend, but for a time he acted as a kind of literary agent. Longfellow trusted his critical judgment, and Ward arranged for the sale of many of Longfellow's poems.

Longfellow's second book of poems was published in 1841. Called *The Ballads and Other Poems*, it included "The Skeleton in Armor," "The Wreck of the Hesperus," and "The Village Blacksmith." By now, Longfellow was physically and emotionally exhausted. Increased teaching duties combined with his heavy writing schedule and the emotional strain of dealing with Fanny Appleton's rejection, had taken a toll. He requested and got a six-month leave from Harvard for health reasons.

In May 1842, Longfellow sailed for Europe. Seeking to restore his health, he traveled to Germany in order to try the popular water cure—a supervised regimen of diet, exercise, and cold baths. While in Germany, he met and became friends with Ferdinand Freiligrath, a rising young German poet. Freiligrath later translated many of Longfellow's poems into German.

Longfellow remained in Germany until October when he traveled to London. Charles Dickens, who had visited Longfellow in Boston the previous year, insisted that Longfellow stay at his home. Longfellow spent two weeks with Dickens before sailing for home on October 22. During the voyage, he wrote his poems on slavery—poems that greatly pleased both Dickens and Charles Sumner.

Longfellow resumed his teaching duties in November. By this time he was well known. His poetry was selling at a phenomenal rate, and he was considered one of the leading poets of the day. His health had improved, and he was happy to be back in Cambridge with his friends. Although he still lamented Fanny Appleton's rejection, he now seemed resigned to life without her.

Chapter Six

"O, Day Forever Blessed"

In April 1843, Andrew and Katherine Norton hosted a farewell party for Fanny Appleton's brother, Tom, who was leaving for Europe. Longfellow was invited. The professor still visited the Appleton family, but he had made no further attempt to break through Fanny Appleton's cool reserve.

At some point during the Norton party, Longfellow and Fanny found themselves alone in a window seat secluded from the other guests. It was not the first time since their estrangement that they had talked together alone, but those conversations had been kept polite and impersonal.

This night, though, sitting with Fanny in the window nook with the party whirling around them, a bewildered Longfellow gradually perceived a new warmth and friendliness. Fanny told him how lonely she expected to be with her brother gone, then added, "You must come and comfort me, Mr. Longfellow."

Longfellow was thrilled by this sudden encouragement, but he had learned from bitter experience to use restraint. He waited almost a week before calling at Beacon Street. Fanny received him with a cautious friendliness, and they talked about the long-standing rift between them. He wrote her a letter after that visit which she answered on April 17.

Judging from her letter, it appears that Fanny—remembering Longfellow's earlier hasty and inappropriate marriage proposal—had extracted a promise that he would not be so impulsive again. She wrote: "I will put aside all anxiety and fear, trusting upon your *promise....*" She apparently set certain boundaries, perhaps even limiting the frequency of Longfellow's visits.

But whatever rules were imposed, it was Fanny who broke them. On May 10, she sent a note to Longfellow at Craigie House consenting to be his bride.

That evening Longfellow wrote in his journal: "The Tenth of May! Day to be recorded with sunbeams! Day of light and love.... I received Fanny's note, and walked to [her house], amid the blossoms and sunshine and song of birds, with my heart full of gladness and my eyes full of tears! I walked with the speed of an arrow—too restless to sit in a carriage—too impatient and fearful of encountering anyone! O Day forever blessed; that ushered in this *Vita Nova* [new life] of happiness!"

It had been seven years since their first meeting. Why Fanny Appleton waited so long to acknowledge her true feelings for Longfellow remains a mystery. She, herself, did not seem to understand it. "It is only to be marvelled at," she wrote to her brother, "that this blessing did not manifest itself to me long ago, but we have both come to the comforting conclusion that it is best as it is, that our characters have been ripened to. . .receive it with fuller gratitude than if the past experience had been spared us."

If Fanny's reluctance had been due to her anger over

Longfellow's revealing novel that depicted her as Mary Ashburton, and himself as Paul Flemming, then her wedding gift to him expressed her full forgiveness. She gave him the sketchbook she had carried with her on their walks in Switzerland. After having it bound in Moroccan leather, she wrote inside the cover: "Mary Ashburton to Paul Flemming."

Once Longfellow and Fanny resolved their differences, they did not waste any more time. They were married at the Appleton home on July 13, 1843, just three months after reconciling at the Norton's party.

The couple spent two weeks in seclusion at Longfellow's rooms in Craigie House and then visited the Longfellow family in Portland. Zilpah Longfellow had feared that her son was marrying a snobbish society woman. But Fanny, whose own mother had died when Fanny was only sixteen, quickly set Zilpah's mind at ease. They sat late into the night talking and getting to know one another. Fanny took great pleasure in seeing Deering's Woods and other local places where she could picture her husband as a boy. After Portland, the newlyweds continued on a wedding journey through the Catskill and Berkshire mountains.

Fanny's father was one of the richest men in Boston. But by this time, Longfellow was a highly respected educator. His books were selling well, and he was already becoming known in America and abroad as America's poet laureate. Consequently, Nathan Appleton had made no objections to his daughter's marriage.

And when Longfellow and Fanny returned to Cambridge from their wedding trip, Appleton bought Craigie House and

Fanny Appleton, as she looked at the time of her mariage to Longfellow.

presented the mansion as a wedding gift. They called it "Castle Craigie."

Longfellow had loved Mary, the wife of his youth, but in Fanny Appleton he found his true soul mate. An intelligent woman with definite opinions, she never allowed her own individuality to be lost in her husband's fame. Her ideas inspired some of his best poems.

When Fanny observed that the line of gun barrels in the arsenal near Portland reminded her of "organ-pipes for that fearful musician Death to play upon," Longfellow was moved to write "The Arsenal at Springfield," using Fanny's imagery. It was one of his most critically acclaimed poems.

Fanny needed all of her strength and abilities to adjust to the swift changes in her life. She rapidly went from reluctant lover to bride to expectant mother, for soon after the wedding, she became pregnant. In February, seven months after her marriage, Fanny wrote in her journal: "I have outgrown my wedding dress, and it will no longer cover one beating heart only!"

Longfellow returned to his teaching duties and also resumed editing the huge volume of poems he had been working on before his marriage. This project, which would be published as *The Poets and Poetry of Europe*, was designed to introduce Americans to non-English poetry. The book was a natural outgrowth of his teaching. It was a major undertaking because Longfellow translated many of the poems himself.

As early as his student days at Bowdoin college, Longfellow had complained of problems with his eyes. They had been bothering him again prior to his marriage, and working on the anthology of poems caused additional eyestrain.

For three years, Longfellow suffered from near blindness as far as reading and writing were concerned. Fanny acted as his eyes much of that time. To protect his eyes from further strain, he scribbled down translations of poems without looking at the paper. Fanny then re-copied them. And in the evenings she read to him.

Without the help of Fanny and his friend Felton—who wrote many of the author introductions for the book—Longfellow could never have completed *The Poets and Poetry of Europe.* After he sought treatment from an eye specialist in New York, his eyesight gradually improved. But the reason for the problems was never clearly established. He would complain about his eyes throughout his lifetime.

Longfellow's visual difficulties could not dim his happiness with Fanny. Their love grew stronger with the passing of time. A year after their marriage, he wrote in his journal: "Dear Fanny—you grow more beautiful, more precious every hour." And Fanny, watching Longfellow take his sunset row on the river a month before their baby was born, exclaimed: "Can any child excite as strong a passion as this we feel for each other?"

The birth of their son, Charles, on June 9, 1844, answered Fanny's question. The new parents were ecstatic. The following day, Longfellow wrote in his journal: "Mother and child both well, and my heart is light as a feather." One month later, Fanny noted that they had celebrated their one-year anniversary by taking the baby for its first outing. "What a year this day completes!" she wrote. What a golden chain of months and days, and with this diamond clasp, born a month ago!"

Longfellow enjoyed being a father. That he entered into the

new role with such delight was fortunate because the children came quickly. On November 24, 1845—the year after Charley's birth—Longfellow noted in his journal that he had received the proofs of his next book, *The Belfry of Bruges and Other Poems.* "My second boy," he added, "and my fourth volume of poems come into the world about the same time." Ernest Longfellow had been born the day before.

Fanny, who longed for a daughter, confessed to Longfellow's sister Anne that she had been momentarily disappointed that her second child was a boy. But that feeling, she said, had been "*very* short-lived," because Ernest had won her heart almost immediately.

A few days after Ernest was born, Longfellow began a new poem. At first titled "Gabrielle," it would be published as *Evangeline: A Tale of Acadie. Evangeline* was his first long ballad, and the first to use an American historical theme. He credited his friend, Nathaniel Hawthorne, for acquainting him with the legend of the two young lovers separated from each other when their people were deported from Acadia [Nova Scotia] to America.

It took Longfellow over a year to finish *Evangeline* because of other demands on his time. Some of his time went to his family, and that he did not mind. He enjoyed playing with Charley in the snow or pulling him about in his wagon. But other claims on his time were harder to accept.

By now his correspondence was growing burdensome. And as his pen yielded an increasingly abundant outpouring of poetry, he felt the burden of teaching grow heavier. On October 11, 1846, he wrote in despair: "All my hours and days go to

Charles Appleton Longfellow

Ernest Wadsworth Longfellow

perishable things. College takes half the time; and other people, with their interminable letters and poems and requests and demands take the rest. I have hardly a moment to think of my own writings. . . ."

Nevertheless, the February 27, 1847, entry in his journal reads: "*Evangeline* is ended. I wrote the last lines this morning." And on the very next day, he began *Kavanagh*, a new novel that would be his last attempt at writing prose.

The Longfellows' happiness was complete when on April 7 Fanny gave birth to a little girl. She allowed her doctor to use the new anesthetic, ether, during the birth. She was the first woman in America to do so. People—even Longfellow's family—criticized her for this.

She wrote to Longfellow's sister Anne: "I am very sorry you all thought me so rash and naughty in trying the ether. Henry's faith [in it] gave me courage. . . ." And she added, "I feel proud to be the pioneer to [attain] less suffering for poor, weak womankind."

Toward the end of the year, Longfellow wrote to Freiligrath, his poet friend in Germany, with a family update:

"Charley the oldest boy is three years old, lithe and limber and straight as an Indian. . . . He is very wild and wilful, and rather disposed to *bully* his mother. Ernest is two years old. .a quiet, gentle boy, with large, soft brown eyes. . . . The baby— Fanny by name—is six months old—round and rosy and soft— like all babies."

Thus ended the year 1847. Surely 1848 could bring nothing but happiness to Castle Craigie.

Chapter Seven

"The Air is Full of Farewells"

The new year began, as the old one had ended, with the sound of children's laughter. If the future cast a shadow, no one in Castle Craige felt its chill. Longfellow resumed his college lectures, saw *Evangeline* go into its sixth edition, and put the finishing touches on his novel. There were visits from Felton and Hawthorne, sledding afternoons with Charley, and evenings spent with Fanny reading a new novel called *Jane Eyre*.

Fanny Longfellow replaced her personal diary with "A Chronicle of the Children of Craigie Castle" that would eventually fill several volumes. The little boys were thriving, and Baby Fanny had stolen her parents' hearts.

The winter days, warmed by friends and family, sped by. Winter turned to spring and spring to summer. On August 30, the first ominous note sounded.

Longfellow wrote in his journal: "Little Fanny is quite ill. . . ." Two days later he noted: "When a child is ill in a house all the usual course of things is interrupted. All thoughts centre in the little patient. Ours is better today."

But the baby's improvement did not last. Instead, her condition grew worse. In anguish and despair, Longfellow wrote: "A day of agony; the physicians have no longer any hope; [but] I cannot yet abandon it." At half-past four in the afternoon of the next day, Baby Fanny died.

Longfellow and Fanny were devastated with grief. "It sometimes seems to me as if this blow had paralyzed my feelings for the other children," Longfellow wrote a week later. "Can this be so? No," he decided, "it is but benumbed for a moment."

Fanny struggled to overcome the black depression that enveloped her. As she had done all her life, she turned to her faith for strength. Still, a month after the baby's death, she confessed: "I seem to have lost interest in the future. . . ."

Only time could bring a measure of healing and acceptance to the grieving parents. Meanwhile, they coped with the daily details of living as best they could. Their home continued to be open to friends who came now to offer comfort. Longfellow tried to lose himself in his work, but was not always successful. On November 12, as the year 1848 crept to its sad finish, Longfellow wrote in his journal: "I feel very sad to-day. I miss very much my dear little Fanny. An inappeasable longing to see her comes over me at times, which I can hardly control."

Longfellow's grief was compounded by a deep concern for his older brother. Stephen was suffering from alcoholism. He had no money and his marriage was crumbling. Gold had just been discovered in California, and Stephen—seeking a new start—meant to go there. During the first four months of 1849 while he waited for a ship, he lived at Craigie House. Longfellow, who had agreed to loan him the money for the trip, soon realized that Stephen was in no condition to undertake such a venture.

Longfellow as he looked around the time of his marriage to Fanny
Appleton.

In April, Longfellow wrote his younger brother Alex that he had arranged for Stephen to be treated by a doctor who "has had such cases before, and has treated them successfully." Longfellow, always generous with his family, paid for Stephen's treatment.

Longfellow also wanted to spare their father additional worry. Stephen Longfellow Sr. had been ill for some time. Perhaps remembering his father's past financial sacrifices, Longfellow wrote his sister Anne: "Tell Papa not to be troubled about the means [amount], as it happens to be *perfectly convenient* for me."

Amidst these sorrows and worries, Longfellow continued his work. He finished the novel, *Kavanagh*, and it was published in April. In June, he wrote "The Building of a Ship," a long poem that reflected the nation's growing fear that the Union would be dissolved over the slavery problem. Abraham Lincoln was moved to tears by the poem. "It is a wonderful gift," Lincoln said, "to be able to stir men like that."

In July, Longfellow received a letter from his sister Anne— who had by now taken over most of Zilpah Longfellow's correspondence—stating that their father's condition was critical. Longfellow brought Fanny and the boys to Portland, where they took hotel rooms, so that Longfellow could be near his parents. He kept long vigils at his father's bedside and tried to comfort his mother.

Stephen Longfellow Sr. died on August 3, 1849. "Farewell, O thou good man, thou excellent father!," Longfellow wrote in his journal. After the funeral, Longfellow went to his father's law office. "Here, he toiled on day after day," Longfellow wrote. "The ledger showed his reward, in page after page of unpaid charges. Alas, for a lawyer in a little town!"

Longfellow and his family did not return immediately to Cambridge, but spent the remainder of their summer vacation in Portland. Fanny still grieved over their dead baby. On August 13, Longfellow wrote to Charles Sumner. "Fanny," he said, "improves in strength under the influence of the sea air; but her spirits do not rise. . . . It has been a very sad summer for both of us."

Fanny, however, refused to give in completely to depression. On the same day as Longfellow's letter, she wrote in her chronicle: "The children longed to go to Deering's Woods, 'where papa played when a boy,' so we gave them a picnic there, a lovely fresh afternoon."

The family returned to Cambridge at the end of August to prepare for the fall term at Harvard. Longfellow began work on a new volume of poems titled *The Seaside and the Fireside*. The book would include the popular "The Building of a Ship," as well as "Resignation," a poem that revealed Longfellow's struggle to accept the baby's death.

After *The Seaside and the Fireside* was published in 1850, Longfellow pondered over his next project. He intended it to be his masterpiece. "I long to try a loftier strain," he wrote in his journal in November. It was to be a trilogy dealing with Christianity from its early beginnings and would show the best and worst of medieval life. He began with the second part that was published as *The Golden Legend*. The entire trilogy, titled *Christus, A Mystery*, was not completed until twenty years later, and he was never satisfied with the overall result.

By April 1850, Longfellow had started *The Golden Legend* and was eager to continue working on it. He was understandably upset when Harvard informed him that he would be expected to deliver seventy lectures in the upcoming year. "Seventy lectures!," he wrote. "It will eat up a whole year, and I was just beginning so cheerily on my poem and looking forward to pleasant work on it next year!"

By the time the next term began, however, Longfellow was more concerned about his brother, Stephen, than anything else. Despite medical care and loving support from his family, Stephen's alcoholic deterioration had continued. Finally, and mercifully, his unfulfilled life, which had once held so much promise, ended. He died at the family home in Portland on September 20, 1850.

Two days after Stephen's funeral, Alice Longfellow was born. Longfellow wrote to Fanny's stepmother: "This morning at half past six a daughter made her triumphant entry into Castle Craigie. . . . What a beautiful morning to be born on! with the setting of the moon and the rising of the sun! and all the splendors of the dawn!"

Chapter Eight

"I Have Delivered My Last Lecture"

On January 28, 1851, Longfellow recorded in his journal: "I have fallen into a very unpoetic mood and cannot write." It was a "mood" that would last three years. During 1851, he continued to revise and rewrite *The Golden Legend*, but he wrote nothing new. Longfellow brooded over his lack of creativity and despaired over time consumed by teaching and in answering the hundreds of letters he received from an admiring public.

In the space of two years, Longfellow had lost a child, a father, and a brother. Then in March, he received a telegram that his mother had died suddenly. He left Cambridge immediately to join his brothers and sisters in Portland. Longfellow grieved, but he was comforted by the knowledge that his mother had died peacefully—"a harmonious close to a long life."

Longfellow's long-widowed sister, Anne Longfellow Pierce, continued to live in the Portland family home. Although Longfellow occasionally wrote and received letters from other family members, Anne would become his primary family correspondent.

Returning to Cambridge after the funeral, Longfellow wrote

in his journal: "Life resumes its course." Unfortunately, that "course" did not include writing poetry. "So ends April," he wrote a month later, "that in a poetical view has been utterly unproductive. I seem to have less and less time—and cannot even correct what I have written."

Mercifully, the spring college term finally dragged to a close. And in July, Longfellow and his family left for the nearby resort town of Nahant. There, the days quickly settled into a comfortable rhythm. Longfellow and Fanny took long walks by the sea and played with the children on the beach. But if Longfellow could not write in Cambridge because he had no time, he could not write in Nahant either. On August 7 he wrote in his journal: "The lazy days lag onward. I cannot write."

In the same entry, noting that *The Golden Legend* was ready for publication, Longfellow added dispiritedly: "I have lost all enthusiasm about it. Probably it will fail." He was still dejected on August 29 when he returned to Harvard to arrange his classes for the fall term. "I felt my neck bow," he wrote, "and the pressure of the yoke."

Longfellow undoubtedly shared with Fanny his fear of never regaining his literary powers, but he revealed little of his distress to his family or friends. In the past, he might have shared these feelings with George Greene and Sam Ward. But he no longer corresponded with these two confidants.

Sam Ward had gone to California to restore his lost fortune in the gold fields. And several years earlier, a rift had developed between Greene and Longfellow—apparently over Greene's treatment of, and subsequent divorce from, his wife, Maria.

Longfellow most likely would have unburdened himself to

Fanny Appleton Longfellow in 1852.

Charles Sumner, his closest friend. But Sumner had been elected to the United States Senate, and in November 1851 he left for Washington. The two friends did write many letters back and forth. But Sumner was struggling with political foes over the slavery question, and Longfellow was evidently reluctant to burden him further.

That Longfellow missed his friend's companionship is apparent. Sumner had been a Sunday-dinner regular at Craigie House. "Sunday has come again," Longfellow wrote Sumner on December 5. "I . . .cast a glance out of the window now and then at the gate, I almost expect to see you. . . ."

Longfellow sounded a brighter note in his journal on December 17. "*The Golden Legend* has a great sale. The first edition of thirty-five hundred is nearly gone, and a second of nearly a thousand is now in press." But these sales did not compensate for his continuing inability to write anything new.

Longfellow's final journal entry for 1851 summed up the frustrating year. "In poetry this has not been a productive year with me . . . . I hope that next year will see more accomplished." But the coming year would be as unfruitful as the last.

Still, all was not gloom in Longfellow's life. His journal and letters abound with descriptions of happy times with his family and friends. He wrote of attending plays and concerts, of cozy evenings spent reading aloud with Fanny, and of hours devoted to building snow houses with his children. Yet, all of these pleasures were overshadowed by his inability to write his "songs," as he called his poems.

Meanwhile, Longfellow's love-hate relationship with teaching continued. When he began the fall term in 1852, he wrote: "I have a kind of liking for it, and yet wish it were all over." Teaching, along with family responsibilities and his heavy correspondence, left him little time for writing and none for the contemplative dreaming that made him creative.

Yet, Longfellow could not bring himself to make the final break with teaching. This is difficult to understand because financially, he could well have afforded to retire. However, his father's warnings that no one could make a living from literature may have still haunted him.

In December with the year nearing its end—the second year in a row that he had written nothing—Longfellow despaired: "It seems to me," he wrote, "that I shall never write anything more."

On February 1, 1853, Longfellow wrote in his journal: "In

Alice Mary Longfellow

weariness of spirit and despair of writing anything original, I turned again, to-day, to dear old Dante, and resumed my translation of the *Purgatorio* where I left it in 1843. I find great delight in the work." Throughout his life, Longfellow turned to translating when he was troubled or when inspiration failed him. Translating stimulated his mind and sparked ideas. Yet, he knew that translating was not the entire answer. "It is only a mask to hide my . . .inability to work," he wrote.

Entry after entry in Longfellow's 1853 journal reflected his increasing despair. "This is the most listless, unproductive year of my life," he wrote in March, "and the most indifferent to literature. I hope I shall be roused up again one of these days. But who knows? This may be the end of it." And in April: "Will the old poetic mood come back?"

Longfellow's gloomy journal entries notwithstanding, his

letters displayed good cheer. And a new baby in the house seemed always to raise his spirits. On October 22, 1853, he wrote to Fanny's lifelong friend, Emmeline Austin Wadsworth: "Fanny has a daughter, born this morning a little before sunrise! And when the sun did rise, a splendid rainbow arched the West, right opposite the window. . . ."

Two days later, Longfellow wrote Charles Sumner about the new baby who would be christened Edith. "The soup waited for you yesterday," he wrote. "The roasted partridges waited . . ., the Madeira, and the Brown Berry pears—all waited for the Senator who came not! Moreover . . .a Maiden from far-away, who came on Saturday, and never yet saw a Senator, waited full of curiosity! We had to drink her health without you."

While Baby Edith brought joy to Longfellow, she did not bring with her his seemingly lost poetic inspiration. He ended the year as he had ended the two preceding it. "For 1853," he wrote on December 26, "I have absolutely nothing to show. Really, there has been nothing but the college work. The family absorbs one-half the time and letters and visits take out a huge cantle [portion]."

Finally, Longfellow could endure his barrenness no longer. On February 16, 1854, two weeks before his forty-seventh birthday, he presented his resignation to Harvard. It would become effective at the end of the spring term. On April 19, he wrote in his journal: "I delivered my last lecture—the last I shall ever deliver here or anywhere."

One month later, on May 20, his journal entry read: "A lovely morning. Wrote a poem—'The Ropewalk.'"

Chapter Nine

"Sorrow Seeks Out Such Days As These"

The first six years following Longfellow's retirement from Harvard were serene and happy ones. Although he acknowledged that there was "a good deal of sadness in [separating] from ones former life," he exulted in his new freedom. Escaping from the grinding routine of academic life unleashed a stream of creative ideas.

On June 22, 1854, shortly after his retirement, Longfellow wrote in his journal: "I have . . . hit upon a plan for a poem on the American Indians. . . . It is to weave together their beautiful traditions into a whole." And only three days later, he wrote: "I could not help this evening making a beginning of 'Manabozho,' or whatever the poem is to be called." Within a few days, he changed the title character's name to "Hiawatha."

Longfellow had always been fascinated by Indian lore. Now, each morning he picked up his pen and walked their forest trails, felt the warm breath of the lazy South Wind, Shawondasee, who "brought the tender Indian Summer," sailed in their birch bark canoes, and joined them around their smoky campfires. "Hiawatha," he said, "occupies and delights me."

The first edition of *The Song of Hiawatha* appeared in October 1855. The book was both praised and ridiculed. Many parodies of the poem appeared. Longfellow found these amusing and noted in his journal the ones he liked best. The parodies mattered little, for within five years, *Hiawatha* would sell fifty thousand copies.

Hiawatha caused an uproar in the literary world when a reviewer accused Longfellow of plagiarizing the poem from *Kalevala*, a Finnish epic. Longfellow was incensed. "This is truly one of the greatest literary outrages I ever heard of," he wrote Charles Sumner. "I can give chapter and verse for these Legends. Their chief value is that they are Indian Legends. I know *Kalevala* very well; and that some of its legends resemble the Indian stories preserved by Schoolcraft, is very true, but the idea of making me responsible for that is too ludicrous!"

Publicly, Longfellow remained silent, letting his friends and other literary critics defend him in print. Since there was apparently no substance to the charge, the furor eventually subsided. But the accusation had caused Longfellow much pain and had consumed cherished time. Time that always seemed to be getting away from him.

Leaving Harvard freed Longfellow from teaching duties, but other responsibilities remained. He persisted in trying to assist his nephews who appeared as determined to fail as had their father, Stephen Jr. He had many letters he had to answer and an increasing number of visitors who interrupted his work.

However, Longfellow himself was often to blame for many of the interruptions. He enjoyed the social life both at Craigie House and beyond. Not unaware of this, he chided himself in

Henry Wadsworth Longfellow in 1855.

his journal: "I lead the life of any respectable gentleman, whose time is frittered away with the nothings of every-day existence." For he could not deny that the routine of his daily life was a very pleasant one.

Longfellow began the day in his study where he stood at the upright desk by the southern window and wrote his poems. Afterwards, he might walk to the Old Corner Book Store at the foot of School Street in Boston. There he would likely meet and chat with writer-friends like Nathaniel Hawthorne, Ralph Waldo Emerson or James Russell Lowell. Or if Sumner was in town, the two of them dined together at the Parker House in Boston.

At home, he played with the children, or read to them. He and Fanny entertained famous writers and artists, as well as celebrities like Fanny Kemble, the popular English actress who gave dramatic readings. After 1855, the family always spent July and August at the seaside in Nahant. At least once a year, Longfellow visited Portland.

And now adding to Longfellow's happiness and following close on the heels of Hiawatha came a new baby. Annie Allegra, born on November 8, 1855, would be the Longfellows' last child. Longfellow wrote his brother-in-law Tom Appleton: "There is a little lady up stairs, whom you never saw. . . . She arrived on Thursday last, just at candle-lighting, and is a welcome guest, though a silent one, for the most part."

In a letter wishing Longfellow's brother Sam a happy new year, Fanny reminisced about the old year: "He brought me a new care but a new darling, so I cannot complain of him. She is a dear little thing. . . . I feel [like] a venerable Banyan tree, with all these young shoots springing up round me. . . ." The Longfellows now had two boys and three girls.

The serenity surrounding Craigie House was disrupted on April 3, 1856, when eleven-year-old Charley Longfellow shattered his left hand in a gun accident. The gun exploded in his hand, and Charley lost his left thumb entirely. Fanny wrote to her sister: "[Charley] bought the gun with money he had saved up, [and] Henry had told him only to use percussion-caps with it, but the temptation was too great—he yielded and was severely punished. . . ."

The family had hardly recovered from their anxiety over Charley when news arrived that Charles Sumner had been physically attacked and severely beaten while seated at his Senate desk. Longfellow was both devastated and outraged. He wrote to his friend immediately, voicing his concern and

Anne Allegra Longfellow

Longfellow's study in Craigie House.

offering assistance.

Despite these alarming disruptions, Longfellow persisted with his work. He had begun reading extensively about the Puritans and Quakers. The day before Charley's accident, he had started writing a dramatic Puritan verse drama about Miles Standish. He continued to work on this throughout the rest of the year. However, he was dissatisfied with the finished piece and discarded it. In January 1857, Longfellow wrote Freiligrath in Germany: "This last year was not fruitful in poems to me. Still I hope to make up for it this year. . . ."

As the new year began, Longfellow remained concerned about Charles Sumner, who had still not fully recovered from his injuries. He urged his friend to escape the political scene and seek treatment in Europe. Much to Longfellow's relief Sumner, after being re-elected to Congress in January 1857, followed his advice and left for Europe.

In March, Longfellow joined the Saturday Club. The informal group included mostly literary people, among them Emerson, Lowell, and Oliver Wendell Holmes. They met at the Parker House where they shared long dinners and discussed literature and events of the day.

Throughout most of 1857, Longfellow wrote only short poems. One of the poems, "Santa Filomena"—a tribute to Florence Nightingale—was published in the first issue of the *Atlantic Monthly*, a new magazine edited by James Russell Lowell. Lowell had asked Longfellow to write something for the magazine. Not until the year was almost over did Longfellow return to his Puritan theme.

On December 2, he wrote in his journal: "I began a new

poem, 'Priscilla' to be a kind of Puritan pastoral; the subject, the courtship of Miles Standish. This, I think will be a better treatment of the subject than the dramatic one I wrote some time ago" The next day he said about the poem: "What it will turn out [to be] I do not know; but it gives me pleasure to write; and that I count for something."

Longfellow continued to work on 'Priscilla' in the new year. On March 1, 1858, he recorded in his journal: "Keep in-doors, and work on 'Priscilla,' which I think I shall call 'The Courtship of Miles Standish.'"

On May 10, Longfellow remembered in his journal—as he did every year— the anniversary of the day Fanny agreed to marry him. "A delicious morning like that of 1843. Fifteen years ago! The air laden with the perfume of cherry blossoms, and full of sunshine and songs of birds, as it ought to be."

In June, Longfellow wrote to Sumner in Europe: "I have just finished a Poem of some length, an Idyl of the Old Colony times—a bunch of May-flowers from the Plymouth woods. The title is "The Courtship of Miles Standish."

The Courtship of Miles Standish and Other Poems was published in October 1858. Despite an economic depression in America, the book sold ten thousand copies the day it was published.

Fanny wrote her sister Mary—still living in England—that it was the largest sale a book of poetry ever had. Remarking also on her husband's phenomenal popularity throughout Europe, she added: "I love to think Henry is so well appreciated among strangers. How much more would they think of him if they knew him personally, for the best of him is not in his books as it is with many poets."

The first three years after Longfellow's retirement from Harvard had resulted in the astonishing successes of *Hiawatha* and *Miles Standish*. But Longfellow was not as productive in the next couple of years. And when his pen was idle, he fretted. "Another week gone without a record. I have written nothing but letters," an 1859 journal entry reads.

Yet, that year he did write a number of short poems. "Enceladus," a poem about the struggle for independence in Italy, was published in *Atlantic Monthly*. It was also the year that he wrote "The Children's Hour," a poem dedicated to his daughters: "Grave Alice, and laughing Allegra, and Edith with golden hair."

Also in 1859, both Longfellow and Charles Sumner received honorary degrees from Harvard. And in November, Sumner, who had finally recovered his health, returned from Europe. He resumed his duties in Washington but visited Craigie House as often as he could.

One day in April 1860, Longfellow and Sumner visited the North End of Boston where they climbed the tower of the old North Church. "From the tower," Longfellow wrote in his journal that evening, "were hung the lanterns as a signal that the British troops had left Boston for Concord." The next day he began writing "Paul Revere's Ride."

Writing about Paul Revere would have offered Longfellow a peaceful respite from the problems of his own century. For in light of the impending civil war, the revolutionary days must have seemed almost serene. "Lincoln is elected," Longfellow exulted in his journal on December 3, 1860. "This is a great victory; one can hardly overate its importance. It is the redemption of the country. Freedom is triumphant."

But the country remained in turmoil. On Christmas Eve, Fanny wrote to her sister that South Carolina had seceded from the Union. Undeterred by the threat of war, the Longfellows celebrated Christmas with their annual family traditions. "Not being able to secure the right kind [of Christmas tree] in time," Fanny wrote her brother, Tom, "we illuminated the old lemon tree and it was very pretty with its light foliage, sparkling tapers, and pendant gifts." As she always did, Fanny saw to it that the younger children received a personal letter from Santa Claus.

By 1861, Longfellow had achieved worldwide fame, and in America he was a household name. At age fifty-four, he was enjoying a happy life. The love between him and Fanny grew stronger every year, his children continued to bring him great joy, and he had all the material comforts he could ever want.

America, however, was in trouble. The new year found the country on the brink of civil war. By January 23, Longfellow noted in his journal that six more states had seceded from the Union. In April, Fort Sumter was attacked, and Fanny wrote to her sister, "war is upon us."

Both Longfellow and Fanny were fiercely antislavery—supportive of Lincoln's Republican Party and of the North. "The North could not stand the firing on the flag at Sumter," Longfellow wrote in his journal. But the battlefields were far removed from Cambridge. And like most Northerners, Longfellow and Fanny mistakenly expected the South to be defeated quickly—long before their own sons would be old enough to fight. Neither had any reason to suspect that a personal tragedy unrelated to the war hovered over them.

On May 20, Longfellow unsuspectingly wrote in his journal: "First grand display of buttercups in the grass. How beautiful they are! The purple buds of the lilacs tip the hedges; and the flowery tide of spring sweeps on."

And then on July 7, 1861, Longfellow's life was shattered, broken beyond repair.

On that hot summer afternoon, Fanny Longfellow was following the Victorian custom of sealing locks of her children's hair in small packets. When hot wax dropped onto the filmy summer dress she was wearing, the dress burst into flames. She ran screaming into the library where Longfellow sat reading. Desperately, he tried to extinguish the flames by wrapping her in a rug, but the rug was too small. When he attempted to protect her with his own body, his face and hands were severely burned before the flames could be quenched.

The next day, Fanny, suffering from excruciating pain that was only partially relieved by ether, lapsed into a coma and died. She was buried on July 14, the day after their eighteenth wedding anniversary. Longfellow, suffering from the burns he received and still fading in and out of consciousness, was unable to attend the funeral.

Longfellow's old friend Felton wrote to Charles Sumner, who could not leave Washington: "I have not seen Longfellow. He has seen no one yet [except] his immediate family. I dread to think of him bereaved of Fanny: she was so perfect a companion of his daily existence, and sharer of his glory. But his children remain, and they must fill in part, her place."

Fanny Appleton Longfellow in 1859, two years before her tragic death.

As soon as Longfellow recovered enough physically, he went into seclusion, first at Nahant and then at Craigie House. He stopped writing altogether, not even writing in his journal. After a month, he managed to write Fanny's sister. Mary was doubly grieved because the sisters' father, Nathan Appleton, had died the day after his younger daughter's funeral. Longfellow wrote: "I feel that only you and I knew her thoroughly. You can understand what an inexpressible delight she was to me, always and in all things. I never looked at her without a thrill of pleasure—she never came into a room where I was without my heart beating quicker, nor went out without my feeling that something of the light went with her. I loved her so entirely, and I know she was very happy. . . . My heart aches and bleeds sorely for the poor children."

Chapter Ten

"Aftermath"

After Fanny's death, Longfellow struggled to keep grief from overwhelming him. He gradually resumed some of his correspondence, but in keeping with his private nature he shared little of his emotional pain. Even to Charles Sumner, he could write only: "I have no heart for anything. There is only one thought in my mind. You know what that is; and how joyless, hopeless, aimless my life has become. So we will not speak of it. . . ."

Longfellow also felt the strain of assuming sole parental responsibility for the children. Fortunately, Miss Hannah Davie continued as their governess. Longfellow's sister Anne helped also by arranging frequent visits to Portland for the little girls— visits they anticipated with delight.

Nevertheless, the children now required more of their father's time. Annie Allegra, the youngest was only six years old. But caring for them helped Longfellow cope with his grief, and he tried hard to keep their routine as it had been before the tragedy. On December 25, 1861, six months after Fanny's death, Longfellow wrote in his journal: "How inexpressibly sad are all holidays! But the dear little girls had their Christmas-tree last night; and an unseen presence blessed the scene."

Entry after entry in Longfellow's journal revealed his severe depression. "The days pass in dull monotony. . .," he wrote on February 12, 1862. And the next day, indifferently: "The war goes on." And then on the fourteenth: "The little girls sending and receiving Valentines. Well, it is something to busy one's self with their business, and partake of their joy."

Finally in desperation, he turned once again to translating Dante. "Translated the beautiful Canto XXV of the *Paradiso*," he wrote on February 20. The work helped. A month later he sounded—if not cheerful—at least more at peace: "All the past week, I have been pretty busy upon Dante, quite absorbed." Translating Dante's *Divine Comedy* would occupy much of Longfellow's time for the next four years.

In June, Mrs. Nathan Appleton, Fanny's stepmother, planned a two-week trip to Niagara Falls with her daughter and some friends. She persuaded Longfellow to join them. He took his sons Charley and Erny with him, but he thought his daughters too young to make the trip. He left Edith and Anne Allegra with their Aunt Anne in Portland. He allowed Alice, who was twelve, to stay with a friend and neighbor in Cambridge.

Longfellow worried about the girls and wrote to each of them daily. "I feel rather lonely without my little darlings," he lamented to Edith. And to Anne Allegra: "Did your doll take cold on the rail-road?"

In October 1862, Longfellow returned to writing poetry. He began *Tales of a Wayside Inn*, a series of stories written in verse. A November journal entry reflected Longfellow's reviving interest in life: "A lovely day. . .," he wrote. "Finished the 'Prelude' to the Wayside Inn."

Longfellow began his 1863 journal with a triumphant declaration. "The President's Proclamation for Emancipation of Slaves in the rebel States, goes into effect. A beautiful day," he added, "full of sunshine. . . . May it be symbolical of the Emancipation."

That same month he recorded that Sumner had been re-elected to the Senate, and that his old friend George Greene had visited Craigie House. Despite these signs of healing, Longfellow continued to fight depression. He still refused many social invitations, especially if strangers were to be present. However, new concerns would soon occupy his mind.

On March 14, 1863, Longfellow received a letter from eighteen-year-old Charley saying that he had run off to join the Army. Charley, who was supposed to be in Portland, wrote: "Dear Papa: You know for how long a time I have been wanting to go to the war. I have tried hard to resist the temptation of going without your [permission] but I cannot any longer. I feel it to be my first duty to do what I can for my country. . ."

Longfellow appealed to Sumner for help. He asked his friend to get Charley out of the service. And if not that, then use his influence to have Charley promoted from his enlisted rank of private to that of lieutenant. But Sumner, after talking to Charley's commanding officer, advised Longfellow to let Charley stay in the service and earn his promotion. "I doubt if you could change him. . .," Sumner wrote. "He could not return without mortification [and] that would be worse than any experience before him."

Longfellow reluctantly agreed, and before long Charley was promoted to second lieutenant on his own merit. Longfellow, forgetting his original dismay and annoyance with Charley, was soon proudly referring to him as "my young Lieutenant."

In June when Charley became ill with "Camp Fever" [probably malaria], Longfellow traveled to Washington and kept a two-week vigil at his son's bedside. As soon as Charley was able to travel, Longfellow took him to the summer cottage in Nahant to recuperate.

Charley returned to the battlefield in August. Longfellow worried so much about his son, who was serving in the front lines, that he dreaded going into town and hearing the war news. He kept busy writing his poems, and in November, *Tales of a Wayside Inn* was published.

By this time also, Longfellow was once again corresponding with his old friend, George Greene, and Greene was becoming a frequent visitor at Craigie House. The healing of the old breach between them may have come about because time had softened Longfellow's previous displeasure. Or perhaps Longfellow, in his loneliness, simply turned again to an old friend. Whatever the reasons, the friendship, once resumed, continued throughout the rest of Longfellow's life.

On December 1, four months after Charley returned to the front, Longfellow received a telegram saying Charley had been severely wounded in the face. Longfellow left for Washington immediately, taking Erny with him. Charley *was* badly wounded, but not in the face. "The bullet," Longfellow wrote Greene, "passed through both shoulders, just under the shoulder blades, grazing the back bone, and making a wound a foot long."

After a week, Longfellow could bring Charley home, and in February 1864 Charley was honorably discharged from the Army. But another year would pass before the war itself ended.

In the fall of 1865, with the war over and Charley home safely, Longfellow began revising his translation of Dante's *Divine Comedy*. Seeking help from friends in the Cambridge literary community, Longfellow created an informal group that he called the Dante Club. They met weekly in the library at Craigie House. Longfellow would read aloud from his translation and then ask for criticism and suggestions. They discussed his choice of words and argued over obscure definitions while Longfellow took notes and made corrections.

The evenings ended with a cold supper of turkey or venison accompanied by salads and wine. Longfellow delighted in the sparkling conversation around his table. The Dante Club did more than help Longfellow with his translation. This gathering of old and new friends eased his loneliness and helped him work through the final stages of his lingering grief over Fanny.

During the next two years, Longfellow concentrated on finishing his three-volume translation of *The Divine Comedy*. He completed it in the spring of 1867, two weeks after his sixtieth birthday. That spring also brought Alice Frere from England.

Longfellow had been a relatively young man, only fifty-four, when Fanny died. Although he never came close to re-marrying, he continued to enjoy the company of attractive women. Undoubtedly, there were some who attracted him more than others, but none more than Alice Frere.

Miss Frere was an intelligent and beautiful woman. At age twenty-six, she was thirty-four years younger than Longfellow. She understood and appreciated poetry, and she was infatuated with Longfellow's celebrity status. What exactly passed between them while Alice Frere was in Boston is not known.

However, Longfellow was not a foolish man. Well aware of their age difference, he would have understood that no long-term relationship was likely to result from their mutual attraction. Nevertheless, for a brief period, she made him forget the emptiness of his life without Fanny.

Soon after Alice Frere returned to England, she wrote to Longfellow and gently confessed that she was engaged to be married and had been for three years. He answered her letter with his usual dignity. "I rejoice in your happiness," he wrote, "as though it were my own. . . .I keep very sacred the precious memory of Monday evening. It was the revelation of a beautiful soul, a Song without Words, whose music I shall hear through the rest of my life."

After this brief but intense interlude, Longfellow continued with his life, which as usual centered on work, family and friends. But he grew restless. And the following year, he began considering a trip to Europe with his family. The children were no longer small. Charley and Erny, twenty-four and twenty-three, were involved in their own activities. Erny was to be married in May. And Longfellow's daughters were by now all in their teens. Even the youngest, Annie Allegra, was thirteen.

On May 27, 1868, the family sailed from New York for Liverpool, England. Accompanying Longfellow were his three daughters; Ernest Longfellow and his bride; Charles Longfellow;

The Longfellows and friends preparing to travel to Europe in 1868. Standing, left to right: Samuel Longfellow, Alice Longfellow, Thomas Appleton, Ernest Longfellow, Harriet Longfellow. Seated, left to right: Mary Longfellow Greenleaf, Edith Longfellow, Henry Wadsworth Longfellow, Anne Allegra Longfellow, Anne Longfellow Pierce.

Longfellow's sisters, Anne and Mary; his brother, Sam; Fanny's brother, Tom Appleton; and the governess, Hannah Davie, who had by now become a family friend.

The fifteen-month tour was a triumphant one for Longfellow—filled with honors and recognition of his work. In England, Queen Victoria received him at Windsor Castle. And he received honorary degrees from both Cambridge and Oxford. "Since landing in England I have not had one leisure moment," he wrote to a friend. "I cannot describe to you the overwhelming hospitality. . . ."

But the trip also evoked sad memories. In Switzerland, after seeing Interlaken where he had first met Fanny, he wrote to his friend and publisher, James Fields. "The old familiar places saddened me. They were haunted by too many memories. Interlaken almost killed me. I was glad to get away from it."

And in Italy, he saw things with different eyes than when he had lived there as a student. The enchanted Rome, where Longfellow's father had suspected him of letting love interfere with his studies, no longer existed for him.

On February 15, 1869, eight months into the trip, Longfellow wrote Fields: "I begin to long for my village, and my old friends, and my early dinner!" But he never considered returning home sooner than planned, because the rest of his party were enjoying themselves greatly—especially his daughters, who had never been to Europe.

Finally, on September 13 he could write to George Greene with obvious relief: "We reached home to-day at sunset; and found Cambridge in all its beauty, not a leaf faded."

Chapter Eleven

"As the Evening Twilight Fades"

After returning from Europe, Longfellow gratefully returned to his work. He had, first of all, to answer the huge number of letters that had accumulated during his absence. But in January 1870 he began writing poems for a second volume of *Tales of a Wayside Inn*. Throughout the next two years, he seemed determined to make up for lost time.

Continuing to work on the *Wayside Inn* poems, Longfellow also completed a supplement to the *Poets and Poetry of Europe*, the project that he and Fanny had worked on together when they were first married. And he finished *Christus*, the trilogy he had started before Fanny died.

By 1872, Longfellow's household was growing smaller and his parental duties less. Charley, who seemed to have inherited the wanderlust of his Uncle Tom Appleton, was seldom home. Ernest and his wife had moved into their own house nearby. Only the three girls remained at Craigie House. Each of the children received a bountiful share from their mother's estate when they turned twenty-one. Alice received hers in the fall of 1872, leaving only the two younger daughters still legally under Longfellow's care.

In the last ten years of Longfellow's life, he continued to be creative and productive. In 1874, with his old friend Sam Ward again acting as his agent, Longfellow received $3,000 from the *Weekly Ledger* for his poem, "The Hanging of the Crane." It was an unheard of amount for a single poem. Longfellow wrote to Sumner: "[The publisher] has offered such an enormous price . . .that I am ashamed to say how much it is."

Only weeks after writing that letter, Longfellow received the crushing news that Charles Sumner had died. He had lost other close friends—both Felton and Hawthorne had died several years earlier—but painful as those losses had been, they could not compare to the loss of Sumner, his dearest friend for more than thirty-seven years.

"He was more like a brother than a friend," Longfellow wrote to a friend. Sumner had named Longfellow a trustee of his estate. Longfellow felt a strong responsibility to be worthy of his friend's trust. He devoted many hours to collecting material for Sumner's biography and deciding who should write it.

As Longfellow grew older, he seldom traveled. He was offered large sums of money to undertake lecture tours, but he refused. In 1876 he made a brief visit to Philadelphia to see the Centennial Exposition. After that, his travels consisted only of his yearly visits to Portland and summer vacations at Nahant.

However, Longfellow had resumed some of the social activities he had shunned after Fanny's death. He again attended the Saturday Club regularly, and he continued to entertain his friends and the many visitors from Europe. In his work, he maintained the same steady pace, becoming if anything, more prolific.

This armchair, made from the wood of the Village Chestnut tree, was given to Longfellow by school children on his seventy-second birthday.

On January 10, 1878, Longfellow's oldest daughter, Edith, married Richard Henry Dana II. Longfellow was pleased with her choice, but it was hard for him to let her go. Writing to Fanny's sister Mary after the wedding, he lamented: "I have lost my little Edith. How I shall miss her!"

But less than two years later when Edith presented him with his first grandchild—a little boy—he was overjoyed. Longfellow wrote to George Greene: "He is a nice little boy, and roars lustily in the night. . . ."

On February 27, 1879, Longfellow wrote in his journal: "My seventy-second birthday. A present from the children of Cambridge of a beautiful armchair, made from the wood of the Village Blacksmith's chestnut tree." The gift pleased Longfellow, and he wrote a poem for the children called "From

My Arm-Chair" which was published in the Cambridge newspapers.

Longfellow published his last volume of poems in the fall of 1880. He used a quote from Horace, the Roman writer, as a motto for the book. The motto, which Longfellow quoted in Latin, translated: "I pray that with sound mind I may live out my old age, neither unworthy nor without song." Happily, the words proved prophetic.

In January 1881, Longfellow's second grandson, Henry Wadsworth Longfellow Dana was born. But only three months after that happy event, James Fields died. Fields had not only been a loyal friend for nearly forty years, but as Longfellow's longtime publisher, he had been responsible for much of Longfellow's professional success.

"Another friend gone," Longfellow wrote Greene. "It is a great shock to me. . . ." But Longfellow did not give in to melancholy. He made his annual pilgrimage to Portland in July and then spent the remainder of the summer at Nahant surrounded by his devoted daughters and his grandsons.

Except for painful neuralgia that had plagued him since his last trip to Europe, Longfellow had enjoyed reasonably good health throughout his final years. But in October, after returning to Cambridge, he was stricken with what he described as a "nervous attack." He suffered from vertigo and was confined to his room through December.

Longfellow never regained his physical health, but he remained as mentally alert as ever. Even in his illness he continued to worry about answering all the letters he received. "I sometimes wish I had taken the ground of not answering any," he wrote to Greene, "but that seemed to me too uncivil." As he failed in strength, he dictated his letters to Anne Allegra.

Finally, in order to answer the many letters from strangers, he was forced to resort to a printed form that read: "On account of illness, Mr. Longfellow finds it impossible to answer any letters at present. He can only acknowledge their receipt, and regret his inability to do more."

On the afternoon of March 24, 1882, surrounded by his family, America's most beloved poet died. He was seventy-five years old. Only days before his death, Longfellow had written "The Bells of San Blas," his last poem. The last lines of its closing stanza left a legacy of hope for his grieving public:

> *Out of the shadows of night*
> The world rolls into light;
> *It is daybreak everywhere.*

Notes

Page 12: Wadsworth House eventually became known as the Wadsworth-Longfellow House. Longfellow's sister Anne, who moved back into the family home after being widowed, lived in the house until her death in 1901.

Page 14: There were no high schools in 1820. Academies, established in the latter part of the eighteenth century, served as the primary secondary educational institutions. Depending on the academy, a student either went directly from the academy to college, or began working at a trade learned there.

Page 20: Nathaniel Hawthorne was a Bowdoin classmate of Longfellow's, but they did not become friends until after college.

Page 22: William Browne eventually received his degree in absentia. By June 1825—when Longfellow was nearing graduation—Browne was back in Portland studying for the Law and editing a regular column for the *Portland Advertiser*.

Page 28: During his senior year of college, Longfellow published over forty poems in various magazines and newspapers. Later, when he published his first collection of poems, *Voices of the Night*, he included only seven of these early poems.

Page 32: The classical languages, Greek and Latin, were taught in all universities, but instruction in the so-called modern languages such as French, Italian and Spanish was just beginning.

Page 33. Washington Irving was the first American writer to be read in Europe, as well as in America. Such stories as "Rip Van Winkle" and "The Legend of Sleepy Hollow—the first modern short stories—appeared in *The Sketch Book*.

Page 33. There were no ocean steamers in 1826. It was necessary to take a sailing packet—a small ship like the *Cadmus*—that sailed on a regular schedule and carried mail and merchandise as well as passengers.

Page 46. Longfellow sent the *Outre-Mer* manuscript to his father for review. Stephen Longfellow, fearing no one would understand the title, urged him to change it. Longfellow refused, but he did explain in the book's introduction that pilgrims and crusaders of old had called the Holy Land, the Pays d'Outre-Mer, or the Land beyond the Sea.

Page 48. Young women did not travel without a chaperon in the nineteenth century. Thus, Clara Crowinshield and Mary Goddard agreed to pay Longfellow for acting as their chaperon and guide. He accepted the responsibility willingly, because it would help finance the trip. Miss Crowinshield kept a diary during the journey that was later published in book form.

Page 53. Clara Crowinshield wanted to tour Austria and Switzerland also, but Longfellow could not find a suitable traveling companion for her, and of course she could not travel with Longfellow alone. Longfellow and Clara had met William Cullen Bryant—the premier American poet—and his family in Heidelberg. Clara and Mrs. Bryant become good friends, and Clara remained with the Bryants in Heidelberg while Longfellow set off alone.

Page 56. At one time, Longfellow and Hawthorne considered collaborating on a book of fairy tales for children, but they never carried out the plan.

Page 58. One of the students taking notes at Longfellow's lectures was the future author of *Walden's Pond*, Henry David Thoreau.

Page 63. The antislavery Quaker poet, John Greenleaf Whittier, was so impressed with the slavery poems that he tried to convince Longfellow to run for Congress.

Page 64. Katherine Norton had corresponded with Longfellow regularly while he was in Germany. Fond of both Longfellow and Fanny Appleton, she may have maneuvered the isolated meeting between the two.

Page 66. About fifty people attended the wedding, all in formal dress. Longfellow's sister Anne represented the Longfellow family. Charles Sumner served as Longfellow's best man. Fanny Appleton wore a simple white muslin dress and a bridal veil adorned with natural orange blossoms.

Page 68. The Poets and Poetry of Europe included selections from the literature of ten modern languages. It was the first anthology of its kind, and made an important contribution toward educating Americans in European literature.

Page 70. Hawthorne had heard the story that led to *Evangeline* from a Salem clergyman. The story grew out of the French and Indian wars, when England drove the Acadians out of Canada because they would not fight against the French. Evangeline and her lover were separated, and spent the rest of their lives searching for one another, sometimes passing each other without knowing it. It was not Hawthorne's kind of story, and he told Longfellow to make use of the story if he could. Within ten years, *Evangeline* sold 36,000 copies. It was the most wept over poem in the world.

Page 79. From 1850 on, Longfellow helped his sister, Anne, with expenses. When Stephen Longfellow Jr. died, Anne was awarded legal custody of his third son. Stephen's sons caused Longfellow and his sister as much anxiety as Stephen, himself, had, but Longfellow was generous with them, both financially and emotionally.

Page 80. Nahant was a seaside resort on the coast of Massachusetts, north of Boston. This was the first of many summers that Longfellow and his family spent there. Eventually, Longfellow and Tom Appleton, Fanny's brother, bought a summer cottage together on the south shore.

Page 80. Longfellow had been fond of Maria Greene. In his letters to George Greene, he had always added a personal note to Maria. Details of what happened between the Greenes that caused Longfellow to become so upset with his old friend are obscure.

Page 83. Dante Alighieri was a fourteenth century Italian writer. *Purgatorio* is part of his masterpiece, *The Divine Comedy.*

Page 86. Henry Rowe Schoolcraft was an authority on Indian tribes of the United States. Four volumes of his six-volume work on Native Americans had been published at the time Longfellow wrote *The Song of Hiawatha*.

Page 88. On May 22, 1856, Congressman Preston Smith Brooks of South Carolina, infuriated by a speech given by Charles Sumner two days before, assaulted Sumner. It took Sumner three years to recover from the resulting neck and spinal injuries.

Page 90. James Russell Lowell, a poet in his own right, had been named as Longfellow's replacement at Harvard.

Page 90-91. The Courtship of Miles Standish is based on the folklore of the Plymouth colony, founded in 1620. Miles Standish was the leader of the Plymouth colony. The poem tells how *Mayflower* Pilgrims John Alden and Priscilla Mullins (maternal ancestors of Longfellow), fell in love. But out of friendship, John wooed Priscilla on Captain Miles Standish's behalf instead of himself. The phrase, "Why don't you speak for yourself, John?" which Priscilla spoke to John in the poem became and remains a much used American saying.

Page 96. It was not until eighteen years after Fanny's death that Longfellow could write a poem about her. But he could not bear to publish it, and the sonnet, "A Cross of Snow," was found in his desk after he died. Only then was it published.

Page 98. The setting for *Tales of a Wayside Inn* was an old inn in Sudbury, Massachusetts. In the epic, a group of travelers gathered at the inn to entertain each other with stories, much as Chaucer's pilgrims did in *The Canterbury Tales*. "Paul Revere's Ride" was included as "The Landlord's Tale."

Page 108. It seems fitting that Longfellow's last volume of poems should include a quote from Horace. It was, after all, his translation of one of Horace's poems that had saved him from a lifetime of practicing law.

Page 109. Ten years after Longfellow's death, his bust was placed in the famed Poet's Corner of London's Westminster Abbey. He remains the only non-British poet to be so honored.

Major Works

Outre-Mer: A Pilgrimage beyond the Sea. 2 vols. Boston: Hilliard, Gray (Vol. I), Lilly, Wait (Vol.II), 1833-34.

Hyperion: A Romance. 2 vols. New York: S. Colman, 1839.

Voices of the Night. Cambridge, MA: J. Owen, 1839.

Ballads and Other Poems. Cambridge, MA: J. Owen, 1841.

Poems on Slavery. Cambridge, MA: J. Owen, 1842.

The Spanish Student. Cambridge, MA: J. Owen, 1843.

The Poets and Poetry of Europe. Philadelphia: Carey and Hart, 1845.

The Belfry of Bruges and Other Poems. Cambridge, MA: J. Owen, 1846.

Evangeline, a Tale of Acadie. Boston: Ticknor, 1847.

Kavanagh, a Tale. Boston: Ticknor, Reed, and Fields, 1849.

The Seaside and the Fireside. Boston: Ticknor, Reed, and Fields, 1849.

The Golden Legend. Boston: Ticknor, Reed, and Fields, 1851.

The Song of Hiawatha. Boston: Ticknor and Fields, 1855.

The Courtship of Miles Standish and Other Poems. Boston: Ticknor and Fields, 1858.

Tales of a Wayside Inn. Boston: Ticknor and Fields, 1863.

The Divine Comedy of Dante Alighieri translation. 3 vols. Boston: Ticknor and Fields, 1867.

Flower-de-Luce. Boston: Ticknor and Fields, 1866.

The New England Tragedies. Boston: Ticknor and Fields, 1868.

Christus: A Mystery. 3 vols. Boston: Osgood, 1872.

Aftermath. Boston: Osgood, 1873.

The Hanging of the Crane. Boston: Mifflin, 1874.

The Masque of Pandora and Other Poems. Boston: Osgood, 1875.

Keramos and Other Poems. Boston: Houghton, Osgood, 1878.

Ultima Thule. Boston: Mifflin, 1880.

In the Harbor. Boston: Houghton, Mifflin, 1882.

Michael Angelo. London: Houghton, Mifflin, 1883.

Timeline

1807   Henry Wadsworth Longfellow born in Portland, Maine, February 27.

1821   Passes entrance examinations to Bowdoin College in Brunswick, Maine.

1825   Graduates from Bowdoin.

1826-29 Studies abroad in preparation for professorship at Bowdoin.

1829-35 Professor of Modern Languages at Bowdoin College.

1831   Marries Mary Storer Potter.

1833   Publishes *Outre-Mer, No. I.*

1834   Publishes *Outre-Mer, No. II.*

1835   Resigns from Bowdoin and accepts Professorship of Modern Languages at Harvard in Cambridge, MA.

1835-36 Studies abroad to prepare for Harvard position.

1835   Mary Longfellow dies in Rotterdam.

1836   Begins Harvard professorship.

1839   Publishes *Hyperion* and *Voices of the Night.*

1841   Publishes *Ballads and Other Poems.*

1842   Spends several months in Germany for his health. Writes *Poems on Slavery.*

1843   Marries Fanny Appleton.

1844   Charley Longfellow born.

1845   Publishes *The Poets and Poetry of Europe.* Ernest Longfellow born.

1847   Publishes *Evangeline, A Tale of Acadie.* Daughter, Fanny, born.

1848   Baby Fanny dies.

1849   Publishes *Kavanagh: A Tale.* Father dies.

1850   Publishes *The Seaside and the Fireside.* Stephen Longfellow, Jr. dies. Alice Longfellow born.

1851   Publishes *The Golden Legend.* Mother dies.

1853   Edith Longfellow born.

1854   Resigns from Harvard.
1855   Publishes *The Song of Hiawatha*. Annie Allegra Longfellow
        born.
1858   Publishes *The Courtship of Miles Standish and Other Poems*.
1861   Tragic death of Fanny Appleton Longfellow. Civil War begins.
1863   Charley Longfellow wounded in battle. Publishes first part of
        Tales of a Wayside Inn.
1865   Civil War ends.
1866   Publishes *Flower-de-Luce*.
1868   Publishes *The New England Tragedies*.
1868-69 Tours Europe with family.
1867-70 Translates Dante's *Divine Comedy* (3 vols.).
1871   Publishes second edition of *Poets and Poetry of Europe*.
1872   Publishes *Christus: A Mystery* and second part of *Tales of a
        Wayside Inn*.
1873   Publishes *Aftermath*.
1875   Publishes *The Masque of Pandora and Other Poems*.
1876-79 Edits thirty-one volume anthology *Poems of Places*.
1878   Publishes *Keramos and Other Poems*.
1880   Publishes *Ultima Thule*.
1882   Longfellow dies in Cambridge.
1883   *Michael Angelo* published posthumously.
1884   Bust of Longfellow unveiled in Poets' Corner, Westminster
        Abbey.

Sources

CHAPTER ONE

10 ". . .very stiff piece. . ." Samuel Longfellow, ed., *Life of Henry Wadsworth Longfellow With Extracts From His Journals And Correspondence* (Ticknor and Company, Boston, 1886), Vol. I, 23.

10 ". . .would gladly have sunk. . ." Samuel Longfellow, 23.

10 ". . .the beautiful town. . ." Henry Wadsworth Longfellow, *The Complete Poetical Works of Henry Wadsworth Longfellow* (Houghton, Mifflin And Company, Cambridge, 1884) 171.

17 "We shall have seven. . ." Joyce Butler, "The Longfellows: Another Portland Family" in *Longfellow's Portland and Portland's Longfellow* (Maine Historical Society , 1987) 25.

17 "Stephen and Henry. . ." Butler, 25.

17 "There is now no kind of danger. . ." Lawrence Thompson, *Young Longfellow* (The Macmillan Company, New York, 1938) 17.

CHAPTER TWO

21 "The long succession. . ." Andrew Hilen, ed., *The Letters of Henry Wadsworth Longfellow* (The Belknap Press of Harvard University Press, Cambridge, 1966), Vol.I, 34.

21 "They are a race. . ." Samuel Longfellow, 32.

24 "All has become quiet. . ." Hilen, Vol. I, 43.

24 "I most sincerely hope. . ."Hilen, Vol. I, 43.

25 "I assure you. . ." Hilen, Vol. I, 280.

26 "I am of the opinion. . ." Hilen, Vol. I, 71.

26 ". . .indeed a most splendid. . ." Hilen, Vol. I, 77.

27 "I feel very glad. . ." Hilen, Vol. I, 83.

27 "In thinking to make. . ." Hilen, Vol. I, 89.
27 "I cannot make a lawyer. . ." Hilen, Vol. I, 93.
28 "I wish to know fully. . ." Hilen, Vol. I, 94.
28 ". . .your literary talents. . ." Samuel Longfellow, 46.
28 "Whatever I do study. . ." Samuel Longfellow, 55.
30 "A literary life. . ." Samuel Longfellow, 56.
30 ". . .introducing spirituous. . ." Hilen, Vol. I, 81.
31 "Get through your. . ." *Thompson*, 76.

CHAPTER THREE
33 "I feel as if. . . " Thompson, 87.
33 "I sail for. . ." Hilen, Vol. I, 157.
33 ". . .reached the shores. . ." Hilen, Vol. I, 158.
34 "To my youthful imagination. . ." Henry W. Longfellow, *The Prose Works of Henry Wadsworth Longfellow* (Houghton, Mifflin And Company, Boston, 1883), Vol.I, 11.
34 "After five weeks'. . ." Hilen, Vol. I, 173.
35 ". . .remember that you. . ." Hilen, Vol. I, 205.
35 "You are surrounded with. . ." Thompson, 97.
35 "You over-rate my. . ." Hilen, Vol. I, 182.
35 "The truth is. . ." Hilen, Vol. I, 182.
36 ". . .in order, you know. . ." Hilen, Vol. I, 198.
36 "It was the first time. . ." Hilen, Vol. I, 220.
37 "In saluting a lady. . ." Hilen, Vol. I, 234.
37 "They have most beautiful. . ." Hilen, Vol. I, 219.
37 "I have seen. . ." Thompson, 114.
37 "How much of my. . ." Henry W. Longfellow, 270.
38 "Next to going home. . ." Hilen, Vol. I, 255.
39 "Were they not aware. . ." Hilen, Vol. I, 286.
39 "Do you, then. . ." Hilen, Vol. I, 287.
39 ". . .my friends can. . ." Hilen, Vol. I, 297.
39 ". . .entrenched behind a rampart. . ." Hilen, Vol. I, 305.
40 "My poetic career. . ." Hilen, Vol. I, 305.
40 "I am sorry. . ." Hilen, Vol. I, 321.

CHAPTER FOUR
43 "Buried in the dust. . ." Hilen, Vol. I, 339.
43 "I fancy that if the Judge. . ." Hilen, Vol. I, 346.

44 ". . .placing in my hands. . ." Hilen, Vol. I, 348.
44 "I have aimed higher than this. . ." Hilen, Vol. I, 362.
46 "I mean to turn author. . ." Hilen, Vol. I, 402.
46 "I am writing a book. . ." Hilen, Vol. I, 408.
46 ". . .the first [part] of Outre-Mer." Hilen, Vol. I, 461.
47 "The students are so much. . ." Thompson, 196.
48 "So here it comes at last." Thompson, 205.
48 "Good fortune comes. . ." Hilen, Vol. I, 459.
48 "We go [to Europe]. . ." Hilen, Vol. I, 480.
49 "I am slowly picking up crumbs. . ." Thompson, 219.
50 "My poor Mary. . ." Thompson, 223.
50 "This morning between one. . ." Thompson, 223.
50 "I cannot study. . ." Newton Arvin, *Longfellow, His Life and Work* (Little, Brown and Company, Boston, 1962) 32.
52 "Traveling is not. . ." Hilen, Vol. I, 566.
52 "There was not one discordant note. . ." Thompson, 237.
53 "It was delightful." Thompson, 235.
53 "Miss Mr. L. considerably." Edward Wagenknecht, *Mrs. Longfellow: Selected Letters and Journals of Fanny Appleton Longfellow (1817-1861)* (Longmans, Green and Co., New York, 1956) 36.

CHAPTER FIVE
54 ". . .a whole year's delirium. . ." Hilen, Vol. II, 161.
55 ". . .a kind of Valentine. . ." Hilen, Vol. II, 6.
55 ". . .serve as a German lesson. . ." Hilen, Vol. II, 6.
56 ". . .from the hand. . ." Thompson, 246.
59 "I have no merriment in my life." Hilen, Vol. II, 59.
59 ". . .the poem being a voice. . ." Samuel Longfellow, 290.
60 "I have not got over it." Hilen, Vol. II, 159.
60 ". . .there is no betrayal. . ." Hilen, Vol. II, 160.
60 "Don't make me [the subject]. . ." Wagenknecht 63.
61 "You do not know how grandly. . ." Samuel Longfellow, 338.
61 "The Prof has collected. . ." Wagenknecht 63.
61 "I sat by my fire. . ." Samuel Longfellow, 338.
61 "The *natural ballad* is a virgin soil. . ." Hilen, Vol. II, 203.
62 ". . .the fourth is now printing." Hilen, Vol. II, 273.
62 "At present, my dear friend. . ." Hilen, Vol. II, 268.

CHAPTER SIX

64 "You must come and comfort me. . ." Wagonknecht, 83.
65 "I will put aside. . ." Wagonknecht, 84.
65 "The Tenth of May! Day to be recorded. . ." Hilen, Vol. II, 487.
65 "It is only to be marvelled at. . ." Wagonknecht, 85.
66 "Mary Ashburton to Paul Flemming" Thompson, 342.
68 ". . .organ-pipes for that fearful. . ." Wagonknecht, 91.
68 "I have outgrown. . ." Wagonknecht, 107
69 "Dear Fanny. . ." Hilen, Vol. III, 19.
69 "Can any child excite. . ." Wagonknecht, 112.
69 "Mother and child both well. . ." Hilen, Vol. III, 19.
69 "What a year this day. . ." Wagonknecht, 114.
70 "My second boy. . ." Samuel Longfellow, Vol. II, 24.
70 ". . .*very* short-lived." Wagonknecht, 121.
70 "All my hours and days. . ." Samuel Longfellow, Vol. II, 59.
72 "*Evangeline* is ended. I wrote. . ." Samuel Longfellow, Vol. II, 81.
72 "I am very sorry. . ." Wagonknecht, 130.
72 "Charley the oldest boy. . ." Hilen, Vol. III, 142.

CHAPTER SEVEN

73 "Little Fanny is quite ill. . . ." Samuel Longfellow, Vol. II, 122.
73 "When a child is ill. . ." Samuel Longfellow, Vol. II, 122.
74 "A day of agony. . ." Samuel Longfellow, Vol. II, 123.
74 "It sometimes seems. . ." Samuel Longfellow, Vol. II, 123.
74 "I seem to have lost interest. . ." Wagonknecht, 143.
74 "I feel very sad. . ." Samuel Longfellow, Vol. II, 128.
76 ". . .has had such cases before. . ." Hilen, Vol. III, 193.
76 "Tell Papa not to be troubled. . ." Hilen, Vol. III, 194.
76 "It is a wonderful gift. . ." Edward Wagenknecht, *Henry Wadsworth Longfellow, Portrait of an American Humanist* (Oxford University Press, New York, l966), 148.
76 "Farewell, O thou good man. . ." Samuel Longfellow, Vol. II, 145.
76 "Here he toiled on. . ." Samuel Longfellow, Vol. II, 145.
77 "Fanny improves in strength. . ." Hilen, Vol. III, 209.
77 "The children longed . . ." Wagenknecht, *Mrs. Longfellow. . .,* 157.
77 "I long to try. . ." Samuel Longfellow, Vol. II, 151.
78 "Seventy lectures! It will eat up. . ."Samuel Longfellow, Vol. II, 165.
78 "This morning at half past six. . ." Hilen, Vol. III, 269-70.

CHAPTER EIGHT

79 "I have fallen into. . ." Samuel Longfellow, Vol. II, 188.
79 ". . .a harmonious close. . ." Samuel Longfellow, Vol. II, 191.
80 "Life resumes its course." Samuel Longfellow, Vol. II, 191.
80 "So ends April. . ." Hilen, Vol. III, 285.
80 "The lazy days lag. . ." Samuel Longfellow, Vol. II, 200.
80 "I have lost all enthusiasm. . ." Samuel Longfellow, Vol. II, 200.
80 "I felt my neck bow. . ." Samuel Longfellow, Vol. II, 201.
81 "Sunday has come again. . ." Samuel Longfellow, Vol. II, 209.
81 *"The Golden Legend* has. . ." Samuel Longfellow, Vol. II, 210.
82 "In poetry this has not been. . ." Samuel Longfellow, Vol. II, 212.
82 "I have a kind of liking. . ." Samuel Longfellow, Vol. II, 226.
82 "It seems to me. . ." Samuel Longfellow, Vol. II, 229.
82 "In weariness of spirit. . ." Samuel Longfellow, Vol. II, 232.
83 "It is only a mask. . ." Hilen, Vol. III, 286.
83 "This is the most listless. . ." Hilen, Vol. III, 285.
83 "Will the old poetic mood. . ." Samuel Longfellow, Vol. II, 234.
84 "Fanny has a daughter. . ." Hilen, Vol. III, 397.
84 "The soup waited for you. . ." Hilen, Vol. III, 397.
84 "For 1853, I have absolutely. . ."Samuel Longfellow, Vol. II, 238.
84 "I delivered my last lecture. . ." Samuel Longfellow, Vol. II, 243.
84 "A lovely morning." Samuel Longfellow, Vol. II, 245.

CHAPTER NINE

85 ". . .a good deal of sadness. . ." Samuel Longfellow, Vol. II, 250.
85 "I have hit upon a plan. . . " Samuel Longfellow, Vol. II, 247-48.
85 "I could not help. . . " Samuel Longfellow, Vol. II, 248.
85 "Hiawatha occupies and delights me." Samuel Longfellow, Vol. II, 251.
86 "This is truly one of the greatest. . . " Hilen, Vol. III, 506.
87 "I lead the life. . ." Hilen, Vol. IV, 4.
88 "There is a little lady up stairs. . ." Hilen, Vol. III, 501
88 "He brought me a new care. . ." Wagenknecht, *Mrs. Longfellow*,202.
88 "[Charley] bought the gun. . ." Wagenknecht, *Mrs. Longfellow*, 204
90 "This last year was not fruitful. . ."Samuel Longfellow, Vol. II, 293.
90 "I began a new poem. . ." Samuel Longfellow, Vol. II, 310-11.
91 "What it will turn out to be. . ." Samuel Longfellow, Vol. II, 311.
91 "Keep in-doors, and work. . ." Samuel Longfellow, Vol. II, 314.

91 "A delicious morning. . ." Samuel Longfellow, Vol. II, 316.
91 "I have just finished. . ." Hilen, Vol. IV, 82.
91 "I love to think Henry is. . ." Wagonknecht, *Mrs. Longfellow*, 213.
92 "Another week gone. . ." Samuel Longfellow, Vol. II, 344.
92 "Grave Alice, and laughing Allegra. . ." Henry W. Longfellow, 176.
92 "From the tower. . ." Samuel Longfellow, Vol. II, 352.
92 "Lincoln is elected. . ." Samuel Longfellow, Vol. II, 358.
93 "Not being able to secure. . ." Wagonknecht, *Mrs. Longfellow*, 230.
93 ". . .war is upon us." Wagonknecht, *Mrs. Longfellow*, 236.
93 "The North could not stand. . ." Samuel Longfellow, Vol. II, 366.
94 "First grand display of buttercups. . ." Samuel Longfelow, Vol. II, 366.
94 "I have not seen Longfellow." Wagonknecht, *Mrs. Longfellow*, 243.
95 "I feel that only you and I knew. . ." Hilen, Vol. IV, 242.

CHAPTER TEN
97 "I have no heart for anything." Hilen, Vol. IV, 260.
97 "How inexpressibly sad. . ." Samuel Longfellow, Vol. II, 371.
98 "The days pass. . ." Samuel Longfellow, Vol. II, 376.
98 "The war goes on." Samuel Longfellow, Vol. II, 376.
98 "The little girls sending. . ." Samuel Longfellow, Vol. II, 376.
98 "Translated the beautiful. . ." Samuel Longfellow, Vol. II, 376.
98 "All the past week. . ." Samuel Longfellow, Vol. II, 378.
98 "I feel rather lonely. . ." Hilen, Vol. IV, 288.
98 "Did your doll take cold. . ." Hilen, Vol. IV, 287.
99 "A lovely day. . ." Samuel Longfellow, Vol. II, 388.
99 "The President's Proclamation. . ." Samuel Longfellow, Vol. II, 390.
99 "Dear Papa" Wagenknecht, *Henry Wadsworth Longfellow*, 180.
99 "I doubt if you could change him. . ." Hilen, Vol. IV, 317.
100". . .my young Lieutenant." Hilen, Vol. IV, 343.
100"The bullet passed through . . ." Hilen, Vol. IV, 372.
102"I rejoice in your happiness. . ." Hilen, Vol. V, 129.
104"Since landing in England. . ." Hilen, Vol. V, 249.
104"The old familiar places. . ." Hilen, Vol. V, 259.
104"I begin to long for. . ." Hilen, Vol. V, 278.
102"We reached home to-day. . ." Hilen, Vol. V, 291.

CHAPTER ELEVEN
106"[The publisher] has offered. . ." Hilen, Vol. V, 713-714.
106"He was more like a brother. . ." Hilen, Vol. V, 734.
107"I have lost my little Edith." Hilen, Vol. VI, 328.
107"He is a nice little boy. . ." Hilen, Vol. VI, 518.
107"My seventy-second birthday." Hilen, Vol. VI, 455.
108"I pray that with sound mind. . ." Hilen, Vol. VI, 599.
108"Another friend gone!" Hilen, Vol. VI, 709
108"I sometimes wish. . ." Hilen, Vol. VI, 779.
109"On account of illness. . ." Hilen, Vol. VI, 750.
109"Out of the shadows. . ." Henry W. Longfellow, 297.

Bibliography

Newton Arvin. *Longfellow, His Life and Work.* Boston: Little, Brown and Company, 1962.

Van Wyck Brooks. *New England Indian Summer, 1865-1915.* New York: E.P. Dutton & Co., Inc., 1940.

J.P.T. Bury, ed. *Romilly's Cambridge Diary, 1832-1842.* Cambridge: Cambridge University Press, 1967.

Helen Archibald Clarke, *Longfellow's Country.* New York: Doubleday, Page & Company, 1913.

Andrew Hilen, ed., *The Diary of Clara Crowinshield: A European Tour with Longfellow, 1835-1836.* Seattle: University of Washington Press, 1956.

Andrew Hilen, ed., *The Letters of Henry Wadsworth Longfellow, Vols. I, II, III, IV, V, VI.* Cambridge, MA: The Belknap Press of Harvard University Press, 1966, 1972, 1982.

Edward Hirsh, *Henry Wadsworth Longfellow.* Minneapolis: University of Minnesota Press, 1964.

Samuel Longfellow, ed., *Life of Henry Wadsworth Longfellow With Extracts From His Journals And Correspondence, Vols. I, II.* Boston: Ticknor and Company, 1886.

Longfellow's Portland and Portland's Longfellow. Maine Historical Society Quarterly, Volume 27, Number 4. Portland, Maine: Maine Historical Society, 1987.

Kenneth S. Lynn, Arno Jewett, eds. *Evangeline, A Tale of Acadie.* Boston: Houghton Mifflin Company, 1962.

Lawrence Thompson. *Young Longfellow.* New York: The Macmillan Company, 1938.

Anthony Thwaite, ed. *Henry Wadsworth Longfellow, Selected Poems.* Great Britain: The Guernsey Press Co. Ltd., 1993.

Edward Wagenknecht. *Henry Wadsworth Longfellow, Portrait of an American Humanist.* New York: Oxford University Press, 1966.

Edward Wagenknecht. *Mrs. Longfellow: Selected Letters and Journals of Fanny Appleton Longfellow (1817-1861).* New York: Longmans, Green and Co., 1956.

Cecil B. Williams. *Henry Wadsworth Longfellow.* New York: Twayne Publishers, Inc., 1964.

Index

Alden, John, 12
Allen, Rev. William, 22
Appleton, Frances, 52
Appleton, Mary, 52, 91, 96, 107
Appleton, Nathan, 52, 54, 66, 96
Appleton, Tom, 52, 64, 88, 93, 104-105
"Arsenal at Springfield, The," 68
Atlantic Monthly, 90, 92

Ballads and Other Poems, The, 62
"Battle of Lovell's Pond, The," 9
Belfry of Bruges and Other Poems, The, 70
"Bells of San Blas, The," 109
Browne, William, 14, 16, 18, 22
Bryant, William Cullen, 28

"Building of a Ship, The," 76-77

"Castles In Spain," 37
"Children's Hour, The, 92
Christus, a Mystery, 77, 105
Cleveland, Henry, 55
Courtship of Miles Standish and Other Poems, The, 91-92
Crowinshield, Clara, 48, 50, 53

Dana II, Richard Henry, 107
Dana, Henry Wadsworth Longfellow, 108
Davie, Hannah, 97, 104
Dickens, Charles, 62-63
Divine Comedy, The, 98, 101
Doane, Carolyn, 26

Emerson, Ralph Waldo, 54, 8, 90
"Enceladus," 92

Evangeline: A Tale of Acadie, 70, 72-73

Everett, Alexander, 44

Felton, Cornelius, 55, 69, 73, 101

Fields, James, 104, 108

Folsom, Charles, 46-47

Freiligrath, Ferdinand, 62, 72, 90

Frere, Alice, 101-102

"From My Armchair," 107-108

Fulton, Robert, 10

Golden Legend, The, 77-81

Greene, George, 38, 43, 46, 48, 52, 59, 61, 80, 99-100, 104, 107-108

Hawthorne, Nathaniel, 56, 70, 87, 106

Hilliard, George, 55

Holmes, Oliver Wendell, 90

Horace, 108

Hyperion, 60

Irving, Washington, 33, 37

Jane Eyre, 73

Jefferson, Thomas, 10

Kalevala, 86

Kavanagh, 72, 76

Kemble, Fanny, 87

Lincoln, Abraham, 76, 92-93

Longfellow, Alice, 78, 92, 103, 105

Longfellow, Anne (sister), 18, 33, 43, 72, 76, 79, 97-98, 104

Longfellow, Annie Allegra, 88, 92, 97-98, 102, 108

Longfellow, Charles, 69-70, 88, 90, 98-102

Longfellow, Edith, 84, 92, 98, 107

Longfellow, Elizabeth, 24, 37-40

Longfellow, Ernest, 70, 72, 98, 100, 102, 105

Longfellow, Fanny (daughter), 72-74

Longfellow, Fanny Appleton, 52-55, 58-66, 68-70, 73-74, 76-77, 80, 82, 84, 87, 90-91, 93-94, 96-97, 101-102, 104-106

Longfellow, Henry Wadsworth
birth, 10
childhood, 13-19
early education, 14, 16-19
student at Bowdoin College, 20-31
publishes first poems, 9-10, 28
travels in Europe, 33-40, 49, 102-104
becomes profesor at Bowdoin College, 42

marries Mary Storer Potter,
44
resigns from Bowdoin
College, 48
death of Mary Storer Potter
Longfellow, 50
becomes professor at
Harvard Univeristy, 54
marries Fanny Appleton, 66
resigns Harvard professorship, 84
death of Fanny Appleton
Longfellow, 94
death, 109
Longfellow, Mary Storer
Potter, 43-44, 46-50, 68
Longfellow, Stephen Jr., 13-
14, 17-21, 24, 30, 34, 36,
74, 78, 86
Longfellow, Stephen Sr., 9-10,
13, 16-18, 24, 26-27, 30-31,
35-36, 38, 76
Longfellow, William, 12
Longfellow, Zilpah, 10, 12-14,
17, 66, 76, 79
Lowell, James Russell, 87, 90

Mead, Rev. Asa, 22, 24
Mullen, Frederic, 9
Mullins, Priscilla, 12

New England Magazine, 44
Newman, Samuel Philips, 25
Nightingale, Florence, 90
North American Review, 44

Norton, Andrew, 64
Norton, Katherine, 64

Orr, Benjamin, 31-32
*Outre-Mer: A Pilgrimage
Beyond the Sea*, 46

Parson, Theophilus, 28, 30-31
"Paul Revere's Ride," 92
Pierce, George Washington,
18-19, 50
*Poets and Poetry of Europe,
The*, 68-69, 105
Portland Gazette, 9
Potter, Barrett, 43-44
Preble, Ned, 14, 16, 18, 39
"Psalm of Life," 59
Purgatorio, 83

Queen Victoria, 104
Quincy, Josiah, 47-48

"Resignation," 77
"Ropewalk, The, 84

"Santa Filomenia," 90
Seaside and the Fireside, The,
77
Song of Hiawatha, The, 85-86,
92
Standish, Miles, 90
Sumner, Charles, 55-56, 63,
77, 81, 84, 86-88, 90-92,
94, 97, 99, 106

Tales of a Wayside Inn, 98-
    100, 105
Ticknor, George, 33, 47-48, 56
Titcomb, Parson Benjamin, 20,
    24
Twice Told Tales, 56

U.S. Literary Gazette, 28, 30

"Village Blacksmith, The," 62
Voices of the Night, 61-62
Wadsworth, Emmeline Austin,
    84
Wadsworth, Peleg, 12-13
Ward, Sam, 62, 80, 106
Wells, George, 27
"Wreck of the Hesperus, The,"
    61-62